the Love Revolution

the Love Revolution

JOYCE MEYER

New York   Boston   Nashville

Copyright © 2009 by Joyce Meyer

FaithWords
Hachette Book Group
237 Park Avenue
New York, NY 10017

Visit our Web site at www.faithwords.com.

Printed in the United States of America

First Edition: September 2009

10 9 8 7 6 5 4 3 2 1

FaithWords is a division of Hachette Book Group, Inc.
The FaithWords name and logo are trademarks of Hachette Book Group, Inc.

Library of Congress Cataloging-in-Publication Data

Meyer, Joyce
The love revolution / Joyce Meyer. — 1st ed.
p. cm.
ISBN 978-0-446-53856-5 (regular edition) — ISBN 978-0-446-55798-6
(large print edition)   1. Christian life.   2. Love—Religious
aspects—Christianity.   3. Helping behavior—Religious aspects—
Christianity.   I. Title.
BV4639.M425 2009
241'.677—dc22
2009020996

CONTENTS

Guest "Love Revolutionary" Writers

INTRODUCTION

Revolution. The word itself sparks hope, ignites passion, and inspires loyalty like no other word in the human vocabulary. Throughout history, the idea of a revolution has poured fuel on firebrands and injected courage in the fainthearted. Revolutions have rallied those in search of a cause larger than themselves and have given previously aimless men and women a cause they were willing to die for. They have birthed great leaders and bred great followers; they have literally changed the world.

A revolution is a sudden, radical, and complete change from the way things are normally done. Revolutions are usually ignited by one person or a very small group of people who are unwilling to continue living the way they have lived in the past. They believe something can and *must* change and they keep promoting their ideas until a groundswell begins and ultimately changes the situation, often in radical ways.

The world has experienced revolutions in the past, as governments known to be taking advantage of their citizens were overthrown. This happened in the American Revolution, the French Revolution, and the Russian Revolution (also called the Bolshevik Revolution), to name a few. Revolutions also took place as outdated, ineffective systems or ways of doing things were replaced and as old ways of thinking gave way to new ideas, such as took place in the Scientific Revolution or the Industrial Revolution. Thomas Jefferson said, "Every generation needs a new revolution," and I believe now is the time for the world's next revolution, the greatest revolution of all. We don't need the same kinds of revolutions that have dotted the landscape of world history in the generations before us; we don't need a revolution based on politics, economies, or technology. We need a Love Revolution.

We need to overthrow the dominance of selfish, self-centered living in our lives. Nothing will change in our world unless each one of us is willing to change. We often wish the world would change without stopping to realize that the condition of the world is the result of the way we live our individual lives and of the choices we make every day.

If every person on the planet knew how to receive and give love, our world would be a radically different place. I think we all know something is wrong in society and that it needs to be fixed, but nobody seems to know what to do or how to begin making changes. Our reaction to a world out of control is to complain and think, *Someone should do something.* We think and say that perhaps God or the government or someone else in authority needs to take action. But the truth is, each one of us has to do something. We must learn to live life from a totally different viewpoint than we have had. We must be willing to learn, to change, and to admit that we are part of the problem.

We cannot fix what we don't understand, so our first need is to locate the root of the problem. Why are the majority of people unhappy? Why is there so much violence in families, neighborhoods, cities, and nations? Why are people so angry? You may be thinking these things happen because of sin. You may say, "People are sinful. That is the problem." I agree in theory, but would like to approach the problem from a practical viewpoint that we all deal with daily. I firmly believe the root of all these issues and many others is selfishness. Selfishness is, of course, the outworking of sin. It is a person saying, "I want what I want and I am going to do whatever I need to do to get it." Sin exists whenever a person goes against God and His ways.

We tend to live "backward"—exactly opposite of the way we should live. We live for ourselves and yet we never seem to end up with what satisfies us. We should live for others and learn the wonderful secret that what we give away comes back to us multiplied many times over. I like the way a famous doctor named Luke put it: "Give away your life; you'll find life given back, but not merely given back—given back with bonus and blessing. Giving, not getting, is the way. Generosity begets generosity" (Luke 6:38 The Message).

In many societies owning, possessing, and controlling have become people's number one goal. Everyone wants to be "number one," which automatically indicates that a lot of people will be disappointed, since only one can be number one at any time in any given area. Only one person can be the number one runner in the world; only one can be the president of the company or the best-known actor or actress on stage or screen. Only one can be the top author or the best painter in the world. While I believe we should all be goal oriented and do our best, I don't believe we should want everything for ourselves and care nothing about other people.

I have lived for sixty-five years at the writing of this book, and I suppose that alone qualifies me to know a few things. At least I have lived long enough to have tried a variety of ways to be happy and have discovered by virtue of elimination what works and what does not. Selfishness does not make life work the way it was intended to work and is definitely not God's will for mankind. I believe I can prove in this book that selfishness is indeed the major problem we face today worldwide and that an aggressive movement to eliminate it is our answer. We need to declare war on selfishness. We need a Love Revolution.

Love must be more than a theory or a word; it has to be action. It must be seen and felt. God is love! Love is and has always been His idea. He came to love us, to teach us how to love Him, and to teach us how to love ourselves and others.

When we do this, life is beautiful; when we don't, nothing works properly. Love is the answer to selfishness because love gives while selfishness takes. We must be delivered from ourselves, and Jesus came for that very purpose, as we see in 2 Corinthians 5:15, "And He died for all, so that all those who live might live no longer to and for themselves, but to and for Him Who died and was raised again for their sake."

Recently, as I was pondering all the terrible problems in the world, such as millions of starving children, AIDS, war, oppression, human trafficking, incest, and much more, I asked God, "How can You stand to see all that goes on in the world and do nothing?" I heard God say in my spirit, "I work through people. I am waiting for My people to rise up and do something."

You may be thinking, as millions of others do, *I know the world has problems, but they are so massive what can I do that will make a difference?* That is exactly the kind of thinking that has kept us paralyzed while evil has continued to triumph. We must stop thinking about what we *cannot* do and begin to do what we *can* do. In this book, I and some guest writers I have invited to join me will share with you many ideas and ways you can be part of a new movement that has the ability to bring radical, positive change.

I refuse to stand by any longer and do nothing while the world spirals downward. I may not be able to solve all the problems I see, but I will do what I can do. My prayer is that you will join me in taking a stand against injustice and be willing to make a radical shift in the way you approach life. Life can no longer be all about what others can do for us, but it must be about what we can do for them.

Every movement needs a motto or a creed to live by. We at Joyce Meyer Ministries have prayerfully crafted a covenant that we have committed to live by. Will you join us?

I take up compassion and **surrender** my excuses.
I stand against injustice
and **commit** to live out simple acts of God's love.
I refuse to do nothing. This is my resolve.
I AM THE LOVE REVOLUTION.

I pray that these words will also become your creed—the new standard by which you live. You must not wait to see what someone else chooses to do, and you dare not wait to see if the movement becomes popular. This is something you must decide for yourself, a commitment you alone must choose to make. Ask yourself: "Will I continue being part of the problem or will I be part of the answer?" I have decided to be part of the answer. Love will be the central theme of my life.

> Ask yourself: "Will I continue being part of the problem or will I be part of the answer?" I have decided to be part of the answer. Love will be the central theme of my life.

What about you? Will you perpetuate the problems in the world today? Will you ignore them or pretend they don't exist? Or will you join the Love Revolution?

the Love Revolution

CHAPTER
1

What in the World Is Wrong?

I am only one, but still I am one, I cannot do everything,
but I can do something and because I cannot do
everything, I will not refuse to do the something I can do.
Edward Everett Hale

While I sit and drink my morning coffee, looking out the window at my beautiful view, 963 million people are hungry.

More than one billion people earn less than one dollar per day.

Thirty thousand children will die today because of poverty. They die in some of the poorest villages on the earth— far removed from the conscience of the world. That means that 210,000 die each week—11 million each year—and most of them are under five years old.

Of the 2.2 billion children in the world, 640 million are without adequate shelter, 400 million without safe drinking water, and 270 million without access to any medical services whatsoever.

Are these statistics as staggering to you as they are to me? I hope so. They are the stunning, sobering facts of life in the world in which we live. These things are happening on our planet and on our watch. I realize the statistics you have just read may not apply to the city or country where you reside, but today more than ever, we are all citizens of the world. We are part of a global community, and members of our human family are suffering in unthinkable, unspeakable ways.

I believe it's time for a worldwide wake-up call—one that will rouse us from our complacency, our ignorance, or our distaste for difficulty and stir us to rise up against pain and poverty, loss and lack, injustice and oppression, and living conditions that don't sustain healthy human life or basic dignity. Indeed, it's time for a Love Revolution.

One Small Mouth, Six Abscessed Teeth

During a Joyce Meyer Ministries medical outreach in Cambodia, a dentist who volunteered his time to go and help pulled twenty-one teeth from a small child; six of the teeth were abscessed. Thinking about this excruciating situation reminds me of the time my husband had a bad toothache while we were traveling to Australia. He was absolutely miserable because he was on an airplane and could get no relief. As soon as we landed, at ten o'clock at night, someone made arrangements for him to see a dentist and he was able to receive help. But what about the little girl and thousands of others like her who endure pain every day and have no access at all to medical care? Take a few moments and imagine it. What would it feel like to have twenty-one teeth that are decayed and throbbing with pain?

This kind of unimaginable suffering exists; it happens to real people every day in remote places of the world. Most of us either don't know about them or, at best, we may see images of some of them on television. We say, "What a shame. Someone really should do something about that," and then we continue drinking our morning coffee and enjoying the view.

Where Trash Is a Treasure

A ten-year-old girl named Gchi lives in a trash dump in Cambodia. She moved there when she was four years old. Her parents could no longer support her, so they asked her older sister to take her, and the only way the two could survive was to live and work in the trash dump. Gchi spends seven days a week digging through the trash with a metal pick or with her hands, looking for food she can eat or for pieces of plastic or glass she could sell to get money for food. She has lived in the dump for six years; many others have been there much longer.

It is vital that you understand that this is the *city trash dump*, and every night the trash and garbage dump trucks back up to the pile of trash to leave the discarded remains of other people's lives, which they have gathered around the city. The children work at night, in the dark, wearing helmets with lights on them because the best garbage is found when it first arrives.

After my visit to that trash dump, an interviewer asked me what I thought about it. As I attempted to articulate my thoughts,

I realized that the situation was so horrible I didn't know *how* to think about it. That depth of degradation simply wouldn't compute in my mind in a way that I could verbalize, but I did resolve that I would try to do something about it.

It took about a year of effort on the part of several people to address the issue and required donations by the partners of our ministry, as well as some of Dave's and my personal finances. But we have managed to retrofit two large buses and turn them into mobile restaurants. They pull up to the trash dump; the children get onto the bus, sit down to a nice meal, and even receive some lessons in reading and math to help prepare them for a better future. Of course, we share the love of Jesus with them, but we don't merely *tell* them they are loved, we *show* them by meeting practical needs in their lives.

Good Intentions Aren't Enough

I heard a story about a man who went to Russia with good intentions of telling people about the love of Jesus Christ. During his visit, many people were starving. When he found a line of people waiting hopefully to get bread for the day, he approached them with gospel tracts in hand and began to walk the line telling them that Jesus loves them and handing each of them a tract with the salvation message on it. To be sure, he was trying to help, but one woman looked into his eyes and said bitterly, "Your words are nice, but they don't fill my empty stomach."

I have learned that some people are hurting too badly to hear the good news that God loves them; they must experience it and one of the best ways for that to happen is for us to meet their practical needs, in addition to telling them they are loved.

We must beware of thinking that words are enough. Jesus certainly preached the good news, but He also went about doing

> We must beware of thinking that words are enough.

good and healing all who were oppressed (see Acts 10:38). Talking is not expensive, nor does it require much effort, but real love is costly. It cost God His only Son, and allowing real love to flow through us will also cost us. Perhaps we will have to invest some time, money, effort, or possessions—but it will cost!

God Is Counting on Us

I am going to leave my home soon to go get coffee with my husband and later we're going to eat lunch. We will probably be gone about two hours, and during that time an estimated 240 children will have been abducted into the sex-trafficking industry. This means two children every minute will have their lives destroyed by someone's selfishness and greed unless we do something. What can we do? We can care; we can be informed; we can pray; and we can take action. We can support ministries and organizations with proven records of rescuing children and women from these horrible conditions, or if God asks us to, we can even choose to work in these arenas. If full-time work is not an option, we can consider doing something on a project basis or taking a short-term mission trip.

Sex Slavery

As you walk down the dark alley, the signs of decay and ruin seep from the darkness. Metal scraps and wire hold the crumbling stone buildings together. The air reeks of rotting garbage and human filth. Behind the deteriorating facade, you hear the wailing cries of a child, muffled shouts of anger and rage, and the shrill howl of one of the many stray dogs that roam these cruel streets.

More than any of your other senses, you are certain of what you feel. There is no doubt . . . this place is evil. As difficult as it is for you to imagine, it is a place created by wicked and immoral men who sell children for sex.

This living hell became Samrawork's home when she was only seven years old. When she was rescued at the bus station at age twelve, she had deteriorated into a lifeless shell of a little girl—skin and bones, emotionally dead with hollow eyes incapable of expression. For five years she was the victim of lustful perverts who paid a higher price for the privilege of violating her little body. They paid three dollars instead of one dollar because she was so young.

The punishment to her female organs was so severe that she would need extensive surgical repair to ever live a normal life. But the immediacy of her physical needs was minor compared to the damage she suffered spiritually and emotionally.

Samrawork has been diagnosed with the HIV virus. An orphan, she has no memory of any parents. Like so many others like her, she is trapped in a darkness of unimaginable evil.

Statistics[1] say:

- 1.2 million children are trafficked every year; this is in addition to the millions already held captive by trafficking.
- Every two minutes a child is being prepared for sexual exploitation.
- Approximately 30 million children have lost their childhood through sexual exploitation over the last thirty years.

The dentist I mentioned earlier in this chapter participated in one of our Joyce Meyer Ministries medical outreaches, which take place in third-world countries. They're staffed by a few people who are on our payroll, but most of them are wonderful volunteers who take time off from work and pay their own expenses to go with us. They work twelve to sixteen hours a day, usually in places where the temperature is much higher than they are accustomed to with no air conditioning and perhaps no fan. They work in remote villages, under tents, and are able to help people who may not have ever received medical care of any kind. We are able to give them life-saving and pain-relieving medicines. We give them vitamins, feed them, and let them know that Jesus does indeed love them. Each one is given an opportunity to receive Jesus, and most of them choose to do so. I get tears in my eyes as I remember the doctors, dentists, nurses, and other medical aides who have told us with great emotion about how these trips changed their lives forever. We try to thank them and they end up thanking us for opening their eyes to what life is really all about.

We took an accountant who works for our ministry on a trip to Cambodia, and although she often sees the media presentations about our outreaches, her life was really impacted by what she saw in person. She said: "I actually feel like I have been living in a bubble all of my life." She meant that she had been isolated from reality, and I think most of us are. I realize that not everyone in the world will be able to go to a third-world country to see firsthand how people there are forced to live, but we can at least try to remember when we read about or see them on television that what we are seeing is actually happening to someone—many someones. God loves these people, and He is counting on us to do something about it.

Malnutrition

Mehret sees the world from a different perspective. In Angacha, a small Ethiopian village, she does her best to keep up with the other children, but she's simply not like all the rest.

Mehret was born healthy, but each day as malnutrition ate away at her body, it caused her spine to grow more crooked, making it difficult to walk, impossible to run and play with friends. It also produced a large growth that protrudes from the right side of her back—too big to hide, and too painful to ignore. Her bones are weak, and so is she.

If anyone knows Mehret's pain, it is her father, Abeba. The one thing he wants more than anything is simply to feed his children...*and make his precious daughter well again.* If

Mehret can begin receiving the nutritious food she needs, the deterioration process can be stopped. But right now, there is no hope in sight.

Day after day, Abeba battles the guilt of not being able to feed his babies. He also knows that if something doesn't change, Mehret's condition will only get worse. Soon, she won't be able to walk. And she will eventually die.

Today, Mehret knows the pain of feeling hungry...and the pain of being different than all of the rest. And she knows that each new day will be a little more difficult than the one before.

In partnership with International Crisis Aid, Joyce Meyer Ministries has begun providing Mehret the food she needs to live and to stop further spinal deterioration. But there are so many more precious young children...so many more like Mehret...who need our help to win this war against malnutrition.

Statistics[2] say:

- Right now, an estimated 963 million people in the world go hungry.
- Every day, almost 16,000 children die from hunger-related causes—one child every five seconds.
- In 2006, about 9.7 million children died before they reached their fifth birthday. Almost all of these deaths occurred in developing countries—four-fifths of them in sub-Saharan Africa and South Asia, the two regions that also suffer from the highest rates of hunger and malnutrition.

A Crack in the World's Foundation

It seems to me that the world system has a crack in its foundation, and we are all sitting idly by and watching it fall apart. If you listen carefully, you will hear people saying it everywhere: "The world is falling apart." We hear it on the news and in general conversation. It seems everyone is talking about the injustice in the world. But talk without action solves nothing. My question is, "Who will revolt against injustice and work to make wrong things right?" I have decided that I will. I know several thousand others who have determined that they will do the same, but we need hundreds of thousands to join us in order to get the job done.

Whatever You Can Do Is Worth Doing

You may be thinking, *Joyce, what I can do won't even make a dent in the problems we have in the world.* I know how you feel, because I once felt the same way. But if we all think that way, nobody will do anything and nothing will change. Although our individual efforts may not solve the problems, together we can make a major difference. God won't hold us accountable for what we could not do, but He will hold us accountable for the things we could have done.

I had recently returned from a trip to India and was at the gym when a woman I often see there asked me if I really believed that all the effort required for these trips was solving anything since millions would still be starving, no matter how many we fed. I shared with her what God placed in my heart—something that forever settled the issue for me. If you or I were hungry because we hadn't eaten in three days and someone offered us one meal that would alleviate the pain in our stomachs for a day, would we take it and be glad to have it? Of course we would. And so are the people we help. We are able to set up continual-care programs for many of them, but there will always be those we can only help once or twice. Still, I know that these outreaches are worth doing. If we can give one hungry child one meal, it is worth doing. If we can help one person go without pain for one day, it is worth doing. I have resolved to always do what I can do and to remember what God said to me, "If you can only relieve someone's pain one time for one hour, it is still worth doing."

The World Has Lost Its Flavor

I think it's safe to say that most of what the world offers is tasteless—and I'm not talking about food. For example, most of the movies Hollywood produces are quite tasteless. A lot of the dialogue and many of the visual images are in poor taste. Usually when we see any type of behavior that is in poor taste we are quick to blame "the world." We might say something like, "What is the world coming to?" Yet the term "the world" merely means the people who live in the world. If the world has lost its flavor, it is because people have become tasteless in their attitudes and actions. Jesus said that we are the salt of the earth, but if salt loses its flavor (its strength and quality), it is good for nothing (see Matt. 5:13). He also said that we are the light of the world and should not hide our light (see Matt. 5:14).

Think of it this way: Each day as you leave your home to go into a dark, tasteless world, you can be the light and flavor it needs. You can bring joy to your workplace by being determined to consistently have a godly attitude. Through simple things like being thankful rather than complaining like most people do, being patient, merciful, quick to forgive offenses, kind, and encouraging. Even simply smiling and being friendly is a way to bring flavor into a tasteless society.

I don't know about you, but I don't like bland food. My husband had a stomach problem once and the doctor put him on a totally bland diet for a few days. As I recall, he didn't even look forward to eating. Dave is not a complainer, but at every meal, I heard him say over and over, "This stuff has no taste at all." It needed a bit of salt, a little spice—and that is exactly what the world needs.

Without love and all of its magnificent qualities, life is tasteless and not worth living. I want you to try an experiment. Just think: *I am going to go out into the world today and spice things up.* Then get your mind set before you ever walk out the door that you are going out as God's ambassador and that your goal is to be a giver, to love people and add good flavor to their lives. You can begin by smiling at the people you encounter throughout the day. A smile is a symbol of acceptance and approval which is something that most of the people in the world desperately need. Deposit yourself with God and trust Him to take care of you while you sow good seed everywhere you go by making decisions that will be a blessing to others.

Change Begins with You

I realize that you can't do everything; I don't question that at all. You must say no to some things or your life will be filled with stress. I am not able to volunteer to tutor children or deliver meals to the elderly, but I am doing lots of other things to make a positive difference in the world. I think the question each of us must answer is, "What am I doing to make someone else's life better?" And perhaps a better question is, "What have I done *today* to make someone else's life better?"

This book may be difficult to read at times because hopefully it will bring up issues that are uncomfortable. But they need to be addressed by each of us. Nothing good ever happens accidentally. If we want to be part of a revolution, that means things must change, and things cannot change unless people do. Each of us must say: Change begins with me!

> Nothing good ever happens accidentally. If we want to be part of a revolution, that means things must change, and things cannot change unless people do. Each of us must say: Change begins with me!

LOVE REVOLUTIONARY
Darlene Zschech

The journey of the heart is one of the most complex mysteries there is. The elation and the sadness, the hoping and the waiting, the highs and the lows...and sadly for many, the unutterable disappointment that literally finds the heart in a place where it functions but does not want to feel anything anymore. When one is without an understanding of the great love of God to lean into and find strength, then the human heart finds a way to cope, to manage, to survive even the harshest of realities. And this is where countless amounts of people find themselves today, from the richest to the poorest, as poverty of the heart does not discriminate where it chooses to find a home.

The prophet Isaiah talked about a radical love revolution in Isaiah 61:11, as the word describes a day in which love would result in people finding their due justice...and Jesus making a way through the wilderness. "For as [surely as] the earth brings forth its shoots, and as a garden causes what is sown in it to spring forth, so [surely] the Lord God will cause rightness and justice and praise to spring forth before all the nations [through the self-fulfilling power of His word]."

A Love Revolution is not only a great idea, but a concept of complete urgency...especially if we are believing to see the tragic injustices happening in the earth today be turned around...including the heaviest tragedy of them all, the tragedy of humanity's broken heart.

The brokenness is brought to our attention again and again

as in the images of a young mother breastfeeding her baby, whose own body is sick and ravaged by the results of HIV/AIDS. She is doing her best but is faced with the choice . . . does she feed her child and knowingly infect her with this killer disease, or does she see the child starve for lack of alternative nutrition? This mum's heart is way beyond broken. She is a mum just like me, filled with delight when given the opportunity to see her child flourish in her care.

To see young men and women just standing around, with no food, no water, nowhere to go and nothing to do, this is heartbreaking to the core and fills hearts with constant disillusionment. Their hearts and minds are full of countless dreams, but if only they could find a way to get to school and buy something to eat.

It's amazing what desperation will cause people to do, causing further harm and extreme violence toward each other . . . how little value people place on a human life when faced with continued extreme poverty. But a heart can only handle so much ache.

A fourteen-year-old boy is raising his younger brother and sister, and younger nephew, in a small tin-covered shack called a home in sub-Saharan Africa, where he works all day on a small crops farm, trying desperately to put them all, including himself, through school and find something for them all to eat to keep them strong every single day. His parents died due to HIV and their town excommunicated the children for the fear that they too had the disease. The odds are high, they are yet to be tested. And this fourteen-year-old extremely brave heart grows fragile due to unrelenting hard work, disease, and uncertainty.

A young mum in Sydney, Australia, who has poured her life into her husband and children, only to find that her husband has been cheating on her for many, many months and wants to marry his new "find." This woman feels isolated, devalued, humiliated, and now has to face a future not only without her husband but also many days without her children as the husband fights for his custody rights. Her heart is so broken that breathing is hard, and she cannot see the way forward.

I remember sitting on the outskirts of Uganda with an incredible leader of one of the stunning child sponsorship programs based there, and as we got to talking, she began to share with me how even though they are doing much to help rescue orphans in that region, the amount of children in their immediate reach who are without the means to survive is overwhelming. I stood up and began to massage her tired shoulders as she continued to speak of her broken heart, and of her unrelenting frustration, and soon the words turned to sobs. Years of living with means stretched as far as they can humanly reach, yet watching and listening as children continue to go to bed hungry and lonely had caught up to this exhausted soul.

The stories could keep coming from here to eternity, of people struggling to survive, from the depths of Africa to highly populated Asia, the US to Oz. It seems that wherever you look, there are major walls of insurmountable heartbreak that even with truckloads of food parcels and immunization, counselors, and community support, we need a lot more to break this treacherous cycle. A LOVE REVOLUTION . . . it is here that we find our life mission.

Luke 4 sends the message out loud and clear:

The spirit of the Lord is upon me BECAUSE
    He has appointed me to preach good news to the poor,
He has sent me to proclaim that captives will be released,

that the blind will see, that the downtrodden will be freed from their oppressors, and that the time of the Lord's favour has come. (See Luke 4:18–19.)

Every time I read and reread this passage, I am reminded to be focused and clear in our endeavors to lift the lives of others...from the smallest of gestures to the grandest of schemes...for this is our time to stand up, walk from the status quo, from a life purely of comfort and self, and stretch ourselves in any way we can to our brothers and sisters in need across the earth.

There is a great word that truly is one of the most powerful words that love actually brings to life...and that word is HOPE. The word says...this hope we have, as an anchor for the soul (see Heb. 6:19)...and Psalm 39:7 says..."And now, Lord, what do I wait for and expect? My hope and expectation are in You." Hope is always alive, even when the situation is bleak or seemingly impossible. Our mission is to bring that hope along with faith and love to hurting people.

My heart has been stretched and challenged to exhaustion trying to come up with answers for those who exist in the midst of some of the worst poverty-stricken environments, but miraculously, as you sit among those who have nothing and situations look hopeless, you do get such a powerful sense of GOD's grace being right in the midst of these wonderful people. Even as they struggle and strain to continue the survival journey, God shines forth again. I have found many "prisoners of hope" as it says in Zechariah 9:12 (I LOVE THAT THOUGHT)...who simply and yet wholeheartedly believe and KNOW that God alone is their answer and provider.

My personal quest, to love the Lord and to worship Him with my whole life, is the highest priority for me in my spiritual life… seeking Him, loving Him, and serving Him. Learning the weightiness of a lifestyle of worship, the value of His presence, and His amazing grace is an indescribable gift and we will certainly need all of eternity to express an adequate THANK YOU for all He has done and continues to do. The learned discipline to bring a song of faith and exult Jesus in the midst of a battle has been one of the great lessons that I have endeavoured to learn in my heart of hearts, but my continued lesson is about what more the Lord is actually requiring of us through worship. And I continually hear His heartbeat throughout the Scriptures on making sure that worship is more than the songs we sing, but as lives poured out, desperate to be His hands and feet on the planet today.

Many years ago, I visited some beautiful African children in an AIDS hospice, all of whom were orphaned, and yet all of whom were filled with the enthusiasm of people who had HOPE. They stood and sang for me…ALL THINGS ARE POSSIBLE, to which I was so challenged and inspired as their little voices filled the atmosphere with life and joy. An unforgettable moment, and an unforgettable reminder of the power of the WORD of God in our lives.

Hebrews 13:15 says this: "Through Him, therefore, let us constantly and at all times offer up to God a sacrifice of praise, which is the fruit of lips that thankfully acknowledge and confess and glorify His name." Verse 16 then goes on to say, "Do not forget or neglect to do kindness and good, to be generous and distribute and contribute to the needy [of the church as embodiment and proof of fellowship], for such sacrifices are pleasing to God."

Singing a God song, joining in the great anthem of eternity, is one of the great joys of life here on Earth. Empowering, defining, we are fueled in His presence to live out the great commission...fueled with our hands outstretched to heaven...and then readied with our hands presented in a stance ready to serve. As Augustine said, "Our lives should be a HALLELUJAH FROM HEAD TO TOE."

However, worship in song alone is only a starting point when it comes to what is required by the Maker of heaven and earth. Over forty times we are instructed to sing new songs, and even more so are we invited to bring offerings and costly obedience before the Lord, but about 2,000 times there are references to being actively involved as our LIVES are presented as an offering, by looking after those who are struggling in various areas of life. It's good to remember, though, that without times of prayer, meditation on the Word of God, and those tender, stunning moments of a deepening relationship with Christ... our acts of service can easily become simply "works based," with the agenda driving the service being about us, rather than being about those who we are serving.

Deliberate times of worship definitely position your heart to be confronted, to yield and be transformed in His presence. Since this whole journey of the Christian walk is a journey of the heart, then you can see why learning to WORSHIP with all you are is a critical step in the process. God has always desired TRUTH when it comes to serving Him...and truth is decided in the framework of your heart, which is why the care and well-being of our hearts is of premium importance where the Lord is concerned.

"Keep your heart with all diligence, For out
of it *spring* the issues of life"
(*Prov. 4:23* NKJV).

I will never forget the challenge that pastor Bill Hybels from Willow Creek Community Church near Chicago gave to us a few years ago, saying that as Christians and Christian leaders, it is not good enough to talk about injustice and watch DVDs about it, he said that we must allow poverty to touch us, to involve us...that the smells and realities of survival become a sense that we never conveniently forget, or even just send money to and feel like we've done our bit. But to be called to action by the great love of God—that we share His love and His life, and that we trust Him to make a way, well, this is the journey we are all called to walk. And this is where our love in action, our worship with our whole lives comes into play.

"And whoever receives and accepts and welcomes
one little child like this for My sake and in My name
receives and accepts and welcomes Me"
(*Matt. 18:5*).

"Who is going to look after my babies?" cries the dying mother, knowing that her children will soon be joining the other multiplied millions across the earth looking for a new mum. I have watched friends with cancer cry out the same prayer. I cannot think of a greater break of the heart, or a deeper groan uttered in the darkest of times. I want to scream out to her. "WE WILL." This is definitely an area where we roll our sleeves up, swallow hard, pray and BELIEVE, and step out in faith. You don't have to live in the third world to find orphans who need a family, or lonely people looking for friendship; each of us lives in cities where children are tossed around government systems that try their best to meet a need that we, the Church, can help meet.

I love the Church...she is so diverse and truly rising across the planet with a new sense of confidence and radiance. But the Church at her finest is when she first and foremost is loving God, with all that she is...and then the Church stands with arms outstretched to serve a hurting community and a broken world, connecting people to Jesus and all that this means. Not judging or criticizing the poor, but simply LOVING...and loving is costly, and is a verb...not a noun. Together, we truly can stand in the gap for those who have no voice...to love the Lord our God with all our heart, soul, mind, and strength...AND to love our neighbours as ourselves. Truly stunning!

So how do we tackle this seeming giant of hopelessness? How do we go about opening a door to those stuck in this dangerous prison?

NONE of us can tackle this on our own. Even the world's most intelligent and interested philanthropists NEED others and the expertise of varied teams of experts who work together for the greater good to have maximum benefit for the most amount of people. But we DO need to make a start; we might sponsor a child, be a voice for those broken in our communities, help some way if you are able in the foster system (e.g., emergency care, short-term or long-term care, weekend buddy systems), raise money for a charity or a need that is in your own heart, get behind the initiatives in your own church and get that body moving, live a little more simply—being mindful of living to give, not just to spend... the list is endless.

But equally important, let's make sure that our own hearts and lives are fueled and alive for whatever opportunity presents itself on a daily basis, whether global or local... just like the story of the good Samaritan, who went beyond the status quo of the day, and actually went out of his way to bring help and answers where others just simply walked by. This Samaritan was MOVED with compassion... and not only was he moved emotionally, but he responded with action.

And may I say that if you are going through a season where you feel you need to be ministered to, rather than being the one giving out, then be encouraged. Surround yourself with an environment of worship and praise, fill your home with music that inspires your heart, fill your car with discs of the Word of God, get around family, church, and community where you know you will be nourished and encouraged... and allow the Spirit of the Lord to fill you continually from the inside out. Whether you need healing, or a financial breakthrough, or a relational miracle... our God is able. Allow yourself to fall into the safe arms of our Lord and our strength, for He will never leave you or forsake you; to trust Him is the greatest joy and hope that you have. But I leave you with this great reminder... to LOVE the Lord your God with all your heart, mind, soul, and strength AND love your neighbor as you love yourself. YOU are completely treasured and valued. Never forget it!

With all my heart,

Darlene Z.

The journey of the heart is one of the most complex mysteries there is—the elation and the sadness, the hoping and the waiting, and for many, the unutterable disappointment that makes us not want to feel anything anymore. When we don't understand the great love of God meant for us to lean into and find strength in, our hearts find other ways to cope, to manage, to survive even the harshest of realities. And this is where many people find themselves today, from the richest to the poorest, as poverty of the heart does not discriminate in its search to find a home.

As Darlene Zschech has reminded us, the prophet Isaiah talked about a radical Love Revolution in Isaiah 61:11, as he described a day in which love would result in people finding their due justice and Jesus would make a way through the wilderness: "For as [surely as] the earth brings forth its shoots, and as a garden causes what is sown in it to spring forth, so surely the Lord will cause righteousness and justice and praise to spring forth before all the nations [through the self-fulfilling power of His word]."

More Than Just a Great Idea

A Love Revolution is not only a great idea but a necessity if we are going to see some of the tragic injustices in the world today turned around, including the heaviest tragedy of all—the tragedy of humanity's broken heart. Psalm 27:3 says: "Though a host encamp against me, my heart shall not fear; though war should rise against me, [even then] in this will I be confident." This is what needs to happen in the hearts of all mankind.

CHAPTER

2

The Root of the Problem

The key to happiness is not being loved,
but having someone to love.
Anonymous

The root of a thing is its very source—its beginning, its underlying support. Roots are usually underground. And because of that we often ignore them and pay attention only to what we see on the surface. A person with a toothache often needs a root canal. The root of the tooth is decayed and must be dealt with or the tooth will never stop hurting. The root of the tooth cannot be seen, but you know it is there because the pain is severe. The world is hurting, and that pain will never stop unless we get to the root of the problems that plague individuals and societies. I believe that root is selfishness.

I've tried to think of a problem that is not rooted in selfishness, and I haven't been able to come up with even one. People think nothing of destroying someone else's life to get what they

> I've tried to think of a problem that is not rooted in selfishness, and I haven't been able to come up with even one.

want or what feels good to them. In a word, selfishness is the source of all the world's troubles.

Selfishness Has Thousands of Faces

Selfishness has thousands of faces, and perhaps that is precisely why we don't recognize it for what it is. We see it in babies who scream when they don't get what they want and in children who take other children's toys. It is evident in our desire to look better than others or to perform better than they do. Selfishness is all about being first in everything, and while there is nothing wrong with wanting to do our best, it is wrong to enjoy seeing others fail so we can succeed.

I believe that all forms of selfishness are bad and that they cause problems. In this section, I want to call your attention to three specific types of selfishness common in the world today and to the negative results they produce.

Sexual Abuse Ann is thirteen years old. Her father tells her she is a woman now and that it is time for her to do what women do. When he is finished showing her what it means to be a woman, she feels ashamed, afraid, and dirty. Although her father assures her that what he does is a good thing, she wonders why he demands that she keep it a secret and why it makes her feel so bad. As the years go by and her father repeatedly molests and rapes her, Ann shuts down emotionally so she does not have to feel the pain any longer. Ann's father has stolen her childhood, her virginity, her innocence, and, without intervention from God, he will have stolen her life—all to get what he wanted.

We are sickened by the incest cases we hear of, but the truth is that 90–95 percent of all incest cases go unreported. I was sexually abused by my father for many years. I tried two different times to tell someone what was happening to me and, since they did not help me, I suffered alone until I was an adult and finally began to share my story and receive healing from God. My father died at eighty-six years of age without ever being formally punished for his crime. The people he worked with, and went to parties and picnics with, never knew he had been raping his daughter since she was a very small girl.

We see what people do and are quick to judge them, but we seldom know the root causes of their behavior. Many women we judge as being "problems in society" are incest victims. For example,

- 66 percent of all prostitutes are victims of sexual child abuse.
- 36.7 percent of all women in prison in the U.S. were abused as children.
- One-third of all abused and neglected children will later abuse and neglect their own children.
- 94 percent of all sexual abuse victims are under the age of twelve the first time they are abused.

The pain caused in our world by incest and sexual abuse alone is shocking, and all of it began because people were selfish and did not care who got hurt as long as they got what they wanted.

Of course, you probably would not kill, steal, lie, or commit violent acts against children, but chances are you are still selfish in certain ways. If we dare to excuse our own selfishness by pointing the finger at those whose crimes are worse than our own, we will never successfully deal with the problems in society today. Each one of us must take responsibility to deal with our own selfish behavior, no matter what level it is on or how we express it.

Greed Selfishness frequently takes the form of greed. Greed is the spirit that is never satisfied and always wants more. Our society today is definitely consumer-oriented. I am amazed when I drive around and see all the strip malls that exist and the ones being constructed. Everywhere we look something is being offered for purchase. Stuff, stuff, and more stuff—and it is all an illusion. It promises an easier life and more happiness, but for many people all it creates is oppressive debt.

The pressure and temptation to purchase more and more just keeps us rooted in selfishness. But, the good news is that we can change if we really want to. Let's learn to buy what we need and some of what we want and then let's learn to give a lot of our possessions, especially ones we are no longer using, to someone who has less than we do. Let us practice giving until it is the first and most natural thing that we do every day of our lives. For the majority of people this would truly be a revolutionary way to live.

The Bible says that the love of money is a root of all evil (see 1 Tim. 6:10). The only reason people love money and will do almost anything to get it is simply that they feel money can get them whatever they want. They believe it can purchase happiness. People regularly kill, steal, and lie for money—and this is all rooted in the disease of selfishness. I recently read an article by a famous actor who said that people believe if they have all the things they want then they will be happy, but it is a false promise. He went on to say that he had everything a man could possibly want and had discovered it still did not make him happy because once a person has reached their goal of owning all the world offers they are still left with themselves.

Divorce Selfishness is also the root cause of divorce. People often get married with the wrong ideas of what marriage should be like. Many of us decide that our spouse is someone who should keep us happy, and when that doesn't happen, the war begins. How different things would be if we got married and set our minds to do all we could do to keep our partner happy!

Right now you may be thinking, *I am not about to do that because I know I would be taken advantage of.* In my earlier years I would have agreed. But after having lived almost a full lifetime, I believe the Bible is true after all. It teaches that love never fails (see 1 Cor. 13:8). It also says that whatever a man sows, "that and that only" is what he will reap (Gal. 6:7). If I believe the Bible, and I do, then I believe that I am in charge of the harvest I receive in my life, because it is based on the seeds I sow. If we sow mercy we reap mercy; if we sow kindness we will reap kindness.

I Was Always on My Mind

When I look back over the forty-two years Dave and I have been married, I am appalled at how selfish I have been, especially in the early years. I can honestly say I did not know any better. In the house where I grew up, all I ever saw was selfishness and I had nobody to teach me differently. Had I known how to be a giver instead of a taker, I am sure the early years of my marriage would have been much better than they were. Because of God in my life, I have seen things turn around and old wounds have been healed, but I wasted a lot of years that I can't get back.

In stark contrast to the way I was raised, Dave grew up in a Christian home. His mother was a godly woman who prayed and taught her children to give. As a result of his upbringing, Dave developed qualities I had never seen in my entire life when I met him. His example has been amazingly valuable to me. Had he not been very patient, which is an aspect of love, I am sure our marriage would not have lasted, but I thank God it did. And after forty-two years of marriage, I can honestly say it gets better all the time. I am happier now than I have ever been because I put more into the relationship than I ever have. I really enjoy seeing Dave do things he enjoys, and that's quite a contrast to all the years I was angry every time I didn't get "my way."

I was always on my mind, and nothing changed until I got sick of my entire life being "all about" me, me, and more of me. Jesus came to open prison doors and set captives free (see Isa. 61:1). He has set me free from many things, the greatest of which is myself. I have been set free from me! I continue to grow daily in this freedom, but I am thankful to realize that real joy is not found in getting my way all the time.

Perhaps, like me, you also had poor examples in life and need to unlearn some things that you learned in your early years. Be honest: How do you respond when you don't get what you want? Do you get angry? Do you grumble and complain? Are you able to trust God to take care of you or do you live in fear that if you don't take care of yourself, nobody will? Believing you have to take care of yourself leads to selfishness, which leads to an unhappy life. I urge you to turn away from selfishness today and begin to value, care for, and truly love others.

Selfishness Is a Choice

Most of us spend a great deal of time thinking, talking about, and making plans for ourselves. Although I strongly teach that we should love ourselves in a balanced way, I don't believe we should be so in love with ourselves that we are the center of our world and all we care about is getting what we want. By all means, we must take care of ourselves because we are extremely valuable to God's plan in the earth. He gave us life so we might enjoy it (see John 10:10). So we need to go for it, but we must not fail to realize that the true path to happiness is giving our lives away rather than trying to keep them for ourselves.

Jesus says that if we want to be His disciples, we must forget ourselves, lose sight of ourselves and all of our own interests and follow Him (see Mark 8:34). Now, I admit that this is a rather scary thought, but I do have an advantage because I have lived long enough to have actually tried it and I have found that it works. Jesus further says that if we will give up the "lower" life (the selfish life) we can have the "higher" life (the unselfish life), but if we keep the lower life we will lose the higher life (see Mark 8:35). He gives us choices concerning how we will live. He tells us what will work well and then lets us decide whether to do it or not. I can remain selfish and so can you, but the good news is that we don't have to. We have the power of God available to us to help us get over ourselves and live to make someone else's life better.

The Journey

Selfishness is not learned behavior; we are born with it. It is an inbred part of our nature. The Bible refers to it as "sin nature." Adam and Eve sinned against God by doing what He told them not to do and the sin principle they established was forever passed to every person who would ever be born. God sent His Son Jesus to die for sins, and to deliver us from them. He came to undo what Adam did. When we accept Jesus as our Savior, He comes to live in our spirit and if we allow that renewed part of us to rule our decisions, we can overcome the sin nature that is in our flesh. It doesn't go away, but the greater One who lives in us helps us overcome it daily (see Gal. 5:16). That does not mean that we never sin, but we can improve and make progress throughout our lives.

I certainly cannot say I have overcome selfishness entirely, and I doubt anyone else can either. To say that would be to say we never sin, since all sin is rooted in some kind of selfishness. I have not overcome selfishness completely, but I have hope of improving daily. I am on a journey and, although I may not arrive, I have determined that when Jesus comes to take me home He will find me pressing toward the goal (see Phil. 3:12–13).

The apostle Paul made the following statement: "It is no longer I who live, but Christ (the Messiah) lives in me" (Gal. 2:20). Paul meant that he was no longer living for himself and his own will, but for God and His will. I was greatly encouraged one day when I discovered through study that Paul made this statement approximately twenty years after his conversion. Learning to live unselfishly was a journey for him, just as it is for everyone else. Paul also said, "I die daily [I face death every day and die to self]" (1 Cor. 15:31). In other words, putting others first was a daily battle and required daily decisions. Each of us must decide how we will live and what we will live for; and there is no better time to do so than right now. You and I have one life to live and one life to give, so the question is: "How then shall we live?" I firmly believe that if each of us does our part to put the welfare of others first then we can see and be part of a revolution that has the potential to change the world.

No Man Is an Island

I am sure you have heard John Donne's famous line, "No man is an island." These words are simply a way of expressing the fact that people need each other and affect each other. Just as my father's life affected me in negative ways and Dave's life affected me in positive ways, our lives can and do affect other people. Jesus told us to love one another because that is the only way the world will know He exists (see John 13:34–35). God is love, and when we show love in our words and actions, we are showing people what God is like. Paul said that we are God's ambassadors, His personal representatives, and that He is making His appeal to the world through us (see 2 Cor. 5:20). Each time I think of that Scripture all I can say is, "Wow! What a privilege and responsibility."

One of the lessons I had to learn in life was that I could not have privilege without responsibility. That is one of the problems in our society today. People want what they are not willing to deserve! Selfishness says, "Give it to me. I want it and I want it now." Wisdom says, "Do not give me anything I am not mature enough to handle properly." The world is lacking in gratitude and in large part, that's because we no longer want to wait or sacrifice for anything. I have found the things I am the most thankful for are the ones for which I had to work hardest and wait longest. Things that come easy usually don't have a lot of value to us.

In many ways, we are raising a generation of children to be selfish because we give them too much too soon. We often buy them a bicycle a year before they can ride it or a car when they turn sixteen. We pay their college bills, buy them houses when they get married, and fill those houses with expensive furniture. Then, when our children end up in financial trouble, if it's at all possible we get them out of it and are there for them every time they need us. We do these things in the name of love, but are we really loving our children or are we just pampering them? Sometimes, by doing these things, parents are trying to "pay" for the time they didn't spend with their children when they were younger. Giving their children lots of things soothes their guilt, and if it's an option, throwing money at them is easy when parents have busy lives.

We all love to bless our children, but we should exercise discipline in how much we do for them. King Solomon advises us to use "wise thoughtfulness" (see Prov. 1:3). At times saying "No" may be the best gift we can give our children because it can help teach them the valuable lessons of privilege and responsibility.

Model Generosity

Model a life of generosity not only in front of your children but also before all of those with whom you have contact. If you are a giver rather than a taker in life, it won't take long before they realize that you are quite different from the people they are accustomed to. Then as they witness your joy, they may be able to connect the dots and realize that giving makes a person happier than being selfish. People are watching, and I am amazed by what they notice and remember.

Paul said to let all men know and see your unselfishness, your considerateness, your forbearing spirit (Phil. 4:5). Jesus encouraged us to let all men see our good and kind deeds so they would recognize and glorify God (see Matt. 5:16). Jesus did not mean that we should be showoffs or do things for the purpose of being seen; He was encouraging us to realize how much we do affect the people around us. Certainly, negative behavior affects others, as I have mentioned, but generosity also affects those around us in very positive ways and makes us happy people.

What about Me?

Right about now, you may be thinking, *What about me? Who is going to do something for me?* This is usually what prevents us from living the way God wants us to live. It always comes back to "me." What about me, what about me, what about me? We are so accustomed to seeing that our desires are satisfied that the very thought of forgetting about ourselves even for one day is frightening. But, if we can manage to muster up the courage to try it, we will be amazed at the freedom and joy we experience.

For most of my life, I woke up every day and lay in bed making plans for myself. I thought of what I wanted and what would be best for me and how I could convince my family and friends to cooperate with my plans. I got up and went about the day with myself on my mind, and each time things did not go my way I became upset, impatient, frustrated and even angry. I thought I was unhappy because I wasn't getting what I wanted, but I was *actually* unhappy because all I did was try to get what I wanted without any real concern for others.

Now that I am discovering that the secret of joy is in giving my life away rather than trying to keep it, my mornings are quite different. This morning, before I began to work on this chapter, I prayed and then took some time to think of all the people I knew I would come into contact with today. I then prayed through Romans 12:1, which speaks of dedicating ourselves to God as living sacrifices, offering up all of our faculties to Him for His use. As I thought of the people I would work with or probably see today, I asked the Lord to show me anything I might do for them. I set my mind to encourage them and be complimentary. Surely we can all find one nice thing to say to each person we meet. Simply trying to do so will help us keep our minds off ourselves. I trust the Lord will lead me as I go about my day.

If you want to dedicate yourself to God so He can use you to love and help others, I suggest you pray like this: "Lord, I offer You my eyes, ears, mouth, hands, feet, heart, finances, gifts, talents, abilities, time, and energy. Use me to be a blessing everywhere I go today."

> "Lord, I offer You my eyes, ears, mouth, hands, feet, heart, finances, gifts, talents, abilities, time, and energy. Use me to be a blessing everywhere I go today."

You will never know the joy of living like this unless you actually try it. I call it a "holy habit," and like all habits, it must be practiced to become one. On some days, I still get all caught up with myself and forget to practice my new habit, but I am quickly reminded when I lose my joy and enthusiasm for life that once again I have gotten off track.

I've been trying to live this way for several years, and it has been quite a battle. The "self life" is deeply ingrained in every fiber of our being and does not die easily. I have read books about love, gone over and over what the Bible says about it, and prayed about it. I have talked with friends about it, preached about it, and done all I can to keep it foremost in my thinking. At times when I realize that I've been selfish again, I don't get upset because getting upset with myself only keeps me involved with me. When I fail, I ask God to forgive me and start fresh; and I believe that's the best policy. We spend far too much time feeling bad about ourselves because of the mistakes we make—and that is a waste of time. Only God can forgive us and He is quite willing to do so if we will simply ask Him.

Yes, I firmly believe the root of the world's problem is selfishness, but it is possible to live in the world and yet refuse to be like the world. If you will join me in starting a Love Revolution, if you will do a radical complete turn-around in how you have been living and aggressively begin to live to love rather than to be loved, then you can be part of the solution rather than part of the problem. Are you ready to start?

CHAPTER
3

Nothing Good Happens Accidentally

I am alert and active, watching over
My word to perform it.
Jeremiah 1:12

None of the revolutions that changed the world happened accidentally. In some cases, they began with just a few people discussing changes that were needed. Whether these history-making events were birthed by casual unrest or well-planned revolt, they never just happened. They were deliberate, intentional, passionate, and strategic. They started because someone refused to do nothing; someone refused to simply "let things unfold"; someone refused to be passive and idle while injustice ran rampant. Revolutions happen because someone decides to act.

Act Now!

The Bible is filled with instructions for us to be active. The direction to be active instead of passive is rather simple, but millions of people totally ignore it. Maybe they think things will get better on their own. They won't. Nothing good happens accidentally. Once I learned that, my life changed for the better.

Wishing for something does not produce the results we desire, but we must aggressively do what needs to be done to achieve them. We will never find a successful man who spent his life wishing for success and attained it. Neither will we find a man who did nothing and somehow became successful. The same principle applies to being part of the Love Revolution. If we want to love people as Jesus instructed, we will have to do so on purpose. It will not happen by accident.

The Bible says we are to *seek* to be kind and good (see 1 Thess. 5:15). *Seek* is a strong word that means "to crave, pursue, and go after." If we seek opportunities, we are sure to find them and that will protect us from being idle and unfruitful. We must ask ourselves if we are alert and active or passive and inactive? God is alert and active! I am glad He is; otherwise, things in our lives would deteriorate rapidly. God not only created the world and everything we see and enjoy in it, He also actively maintains it because He knows that good things do not simply occur; they happen as a result of right action (see Heb. 1:3).

God-inspired, balanced activity keeps us from being idle and unfruitful and thereby serves as a protection for us. Staying active doing right things will prevent us from doing wrong things. It seems we don't have to try very hard to do what is wrong; our human nature drifts in that direction if we don't choose to do what is right.

For example, we don't have to choose disease; all we have to do is be around it and we can catch it. But we must choose health. To be healthy, I have to constantly make good choices about exercise, sleep, and nutrition. I must choose not to worry or be anxious because I know that will make me tired and possibly cause other physical symptoms. To be healthy, I must actively invest in my health, but I can easily get sick by doing absolutely nothing to take care of myself.

The Flesh Is Lazy

The apostle Paul teaches clearly that the flesh is lazy, lustful, and desirous of many sinful things (see Rom. 13:14). Thank God we are more than flesh. We also have a spirit and the spiritual part of a Christian is where the nature of God dwells. God is good and the fact that He lives in us means we have goodness in us. With our spirit we can discipline and rule over the flesh—but it does require effort. It requires cooperation with the Holy Spirit Who strengthens us and enables us to do good things. Paul says we are not to make provision for the flesh and I believe one way we do make provision for it is by simply doing nothing!

Doing nothing is addictive. The more we do nothing, the more we want to do nothing. I am sure you have had the experience of lying around the house all day and found that the more you lay there, the more difficult it was to get up. When you do first get up, everything feels stiff and tired, but as you continue to force yourself to move your energy comes back.

Today I woke up in a rather low mood. I worked hard all weekend doing a conference and am still a bit tired. In addition, I experienced a personal disappointment about something I had hoped for. I felt like lying on the couch and feeling sorry for myself all day, but since I have years of experience doing that and have found it fruitless, I decided to make another choice. I decided to go ahead and write this chapter on activity. It was my way of doing warfare against the way my flesh felt! The longer I write, the better I feel.

In situations where our flesh tempts us to be lazy, we can begin to overcome by asking God to help us and by making determined decisions to be active instead of idle. Then, as we go forward and act on our decisions, we will find that our feelings catch up with them. God has given me a spirit of discipline and self-control just for days like today, but it is up to me to choose whether I use what He has given me or merely follow the ways of the flesh.

Paul also writes about "carnal Christians," who are people who have accepted Jesus Christ as their Savior, but never work with the Holy Spirit to develop spiritual maturity. In 1 Corinthians 3:1–3 Paul told the Christians he had to talk to them as non-spiritual men of the flesh in whom the carnal nature predominated. He could not even teach them strong things but had to stick with what he called "milk messages." He told them they were unspiritual because they allowed ordinary impulses to control them. Do you allow ordinary impulses to control you? I was very tempted today to let ordinary impulses control me and, to be honest, I will probably have to resist the temptation all day long by staying active doing something I believe will bear good fruit. I cannot afford to give in to my feelings because I don't have a day to waste.

No Rewards for Passivity

None of us can afford to waste our time sitting around doing nothing. God does not reward passivity. Passive people do not use their free will to do what they know is right. Instead, they wait to feel like doing something or to be motivated by some mysterious outside force. They wish something good would happen, especially to them, and they are committed to doing nothing while they wait to see if it does. God does not applaud this attitude; in fact, it is actually quite dangerous.

A decision to do nothing is still a decision, and it is one that makes us weaker and weaker. It gives the devil more and more opportunity to control us. Empty space is still a place, and the Word of God teaches that if the devil comes and finds emptiness he quickly occupies the space (see Matt. 12:43–44). Inactivity indicates that we are in agreement with and approve of whatever is going on. After all, if we are doing nothing to change it then we must think whatever is happening is fine.

Do Something

We have taken various people on mission trips to minister to desperately needy people, but they don't all respond the same way. Everyone feels compassion when they see the terrible conditions in which people live in remote villages in Africa, India, or other parts of the world. Many cry; most shake their heads and think these situations are terrible, but they don't all decide to do something to change the conditions. Many pray for God to do something and are glad that our ministry is doing something, yet they never think to seek God aggressively about what they can do themselves. I would venture to say that most of them return home, get busy with their own lives again, and soon forget about what they saw. But thank God there are some individuals who are determined to find ways to make a difference. Remember: Indifference makes an excuse, but love finds a way. Everyone can do something!

> Remember: Indifference makes an excuse, but love finds a way.

I remember a woman who decided she *had* to help in some way. For a while she couldn't figure out what to do because she had no extra money to contribute and she couldn't go live on the mission field. But as she continued to pray about the situation, God encouraged her to look at what she had, not at what she did not have. She realized she was very good at baking cakes, pies, and cookies. So she asked her pastor if she could bake during the week and offer her baked goods for sale on Sundays after church as long as the money went to missions. This became a way for her and other church members to be involved in missions and it kept her active doing something to help someone else.

I also know about a woman who was so desperate to do something that she cut off her beautiful long hair and sold it to help orphans. This may sound rather radical, but I can say for sure that it is much better than doing nothing. Doing nothing is dangerous because it opens doors for the devil to be active in our lives.

Another woman I interviewed is a massage therapist and after attending one of our conferences where I spoke on the need to reach out to others she organized a special spa day and decided all the proceeds would go to help poor people. She raised one thousand dollars for missions and also testified that the day of giving was life changing for her and those who attended. She shared how excited everyone got about working together to help the poor and needy.

We all need to be loved, but I believe our personal joy is strongly connected to loving others. Something beautiful happens in our heart when we give.

Inactivity Invites the Enemy

Lying on the couch or leaning back in the recliner asking God to take care of everything that needs to be done is easy, but it leaves us idle and unfruitful and open to the attack of evil. If our minds are empty of good thoughts, the devil can easily fill them with bad ones. If we are lazy and inactive, he can easily tempt us to do wrong and even sinful things. The Bible tells us quite frequently to be active for it will keep us from being lazy and unfruitful. If we aggressively think about what we can do for others there will be no room in our minds for wrong thoughts.

Idle people easily become discouraged, depressed, and filled with self-pity. They can fall into all kinds of sin. The apostle Paul even said that if a young woman became a widow, she should marry again. Otherwise, she might become an idle gossip and a busybody (see 1 Tim. 5:11–15). Paul actually went so far as to say that some of the younger widows through inactivity had already turned aside to go after Satan. How important is it to remain active? I believe Paul's writings affirm that it is very important.

In fact, throughout Scripture God encourages us not to become inactive. In Old Testament times, when a person died the Israelites were only allowed to mourn that loved one for thirty days (see Deut. 34:8). At first, that might seem insensitive, but God made that law because He knows that prolonged mourning and inactivity can lead to serious problems.

We must stay active—not excessively involved lest we get burnout—but involved enough to keep us going in the right direction. Balance is very important. We cannot spend all our time helping other people, but on the other hand, spending none of it that way creates big problems. If you can think of someone you know who is idle, inactive, and passive you will probably also realize that they are very unhappy because inactivity and lack of joy go together.

Several years ago my aunt needed to move to an assisted living facility. For the first three or four years she wanted to do nothing. She was sad that she had to leave her home and had no desire to participate in the new life that was available to her. Although there were many activities available and even opportunities to help others, she persisted in doing nothing. Day after day she sat in her apartment and was discouraged. She felt bad physically and was often difficult to get along with. She finally made a decision that she couldn't just keep sitting around doing nothing and she got involved in Bible study and visiting patients in the nursing home side of the facility. She played games, went to parties, and made lots of friends. Pretty soon she was telling me that she was happier than she had ever been in her life and felt great physically.

An inactive person's condition goes from bad to worse until his inactivity begins to affect every area of his life. He passively allows himself to be tossed to and fro by his environment and circumstances. He lets his feelings lead him, and since he never feels like doing anything he merely watches and complains as his life falls apart. He wants to do many things, yet he is overwhelmed by a feeling that is almost indescribable. He feels lazy and has no creative ideas. He may even begin to think something is physically wrong with him and that is why he lacks energy. To him, life has become a succession of insurmountable problems.

Allowing ourselves to become inactive often happens after we experience a setback or a series of disappointments, or when tragedy strikes, which I will address at the end of this chapter. When such things occur, we may want to give up, but when we do, Satan is waiting to pounce and take advantage of the situation. We cannot for any reason let passivity give the enemy access to our lives.

Being Active Helps Me Beat a Bad Day

While I'm having my "rough day" today, there are millions of people in the world who would think my day is a party compared to what they're facing. For more than two decades, a rebel army in eastern Africa has been enslaving children by forcing them to be soldiers in a war ignited by a guerrilla militia who has the audacity to call itself the Lord's Resistance Army. These guerrillas terrorize the northern part of Uganda; they kidnap children as young as seven years old and force them to become soldiers or sex slaves, and to do other degrading jobs. Some statistics state that as many as thirty thousand to forty thousand children have been abducted. What began as a rebellion against the ruling government has turned into the slaughter of innocent people by a commander who claims he intends to create a society based on the Ten Commandments, while he violates every one of them.

This man, Joseph Kony, was once a Catholic altar boy. Now he mixes the Old Testament with the Koran and traditional tribal rituals to come up with his own doctrine. His tactics have been brutal. As of this writing, a truce has been called and many of the children are being released, but in most cases their parents have been slaughtered, so they have no homes to go back to. Most of the children have been forced to use drugs and have become addicted to them. They were forced to commit acts of violence that are unbelievable for an adult, let alone a child. Young children have been forced to shoot their entire families. What are they to do now? Wander through the roads filled with rage trying to find a way to forget what they have done. They will need help and I can pray today and ask God to use me. I can get myself off my mind on purpose and think about people like those I have just described—people who have real problems.

I can remember the hopeless looks I saw on the people's faces when I had the privilege of traveling to Uganda and I can continue making every effort to send help to them. I can imagine trying to put a smile on their little faces to replace the anger I saw when I first arrived. I can imagine what their lives can be like after we help build them a new village where they can have adoptive parents, good food, love, and education as well as proper teaching about Jesus and His plan for their lives.

Child Soldier

"Please, God, no more killing. Not today. I can't watch any-more." That is how the prayer went.

Off in the distance, Allen can hear the screams, the piercing blasts of gunfire, and the panic of sheer terror hits him. He knows all too well the significance of the sounds. How could he ever forget? They were the same sounds he heard right before the soldiers stormed his village and violently abducted his mother and father, brutally beating them to death to intimidate and coerce other abductees.

On that horrible day, the rebels did leave Allen behind. But after hiding in the bush for weeks with five other boys, sleeping on the ground with no food or water, the rebels found them. Allen was only ten years old.

From the moment he was abducted, he was beaten two or three times a day and given little food or water. *"Get up, boy. It's time to watch your friends die,"* the rebel soldier yelled to Allen. He was forced to watch helplessly as the soldiers bludgeoned his friends in the head until they lay motionless in a gruesome pool of their own blood. Under threats of death, the rebels forced him to commit heinous acts of evil as well. He could feel his heart slipping into darkness...

Tonight, when Allen is sent to collect firewood, he plans to run. He will run hard...he'll run until he collapses if he has to. Freedom is his dream. And maybe if he runs far enough, he can live for a day with no killing, and perhaps begin to heal.

Allen currently lives in a new village in Gulu, Uganda, designed to house and help child soldiers. Joyce Meyer

Ministries, in partnership with Watoto Ministries, is developing this village to reach affected children.

Statistics say:

- The Lord's Resistance Army (LRA) abducted over thirty thousand children to serve as soldiers or sex slaves in Uganda.[1]
- As of 2007, there were approximately 250,000 child soldiers worldwide.[2]

While I was deciding if I should be down in the dumps all day, I received an e-mail from some friends who have served God in ministry for more than twenty-five years. It's an update on their twenty-two-year-old son, who has very serious, life-threatening thyroid cancer. If I look beyond myself and realize that a great deal is going on in the world besides "me" I gradually begin to feel less absorbed in my problems and more grateful for my blessings.

I'm amazed when I think of how many of our problems are connected to what we think about. As long as I think about what I wanted and did not get, my mood goes down, down, down. But when I think of what I have and the tragedies other people are encountering, I realize that I don't really have a problem at all. Instead of being pathetic I can be thankful!

I am eternally grateful that God keeps reminding me to stay active doing something good, because remember: we overcome evil with good (see Rom. 12:21). Has someone mistreated you? Why not pray for them? It will make you feel better. Have you had a disappointment? Ask God to show you others who are more disappointed than you are and try to encourage them. This will help them and make you feel better all at the same time.

The world is getting more violent all the time. As I continue to write, I have received another message—a text message informing me that a church in another city experienced a random shooting last night. Two people are dead and five injured. I am reminded of what the Bible says in Matthew 24, which discusses signs of the end times and says that amid all the violence and tremendous need, the love of the great body of people will grow cold. This is what we must fight against. We cannot let love disappear because if we do, we are handing the planet over to evil.

When I learned about the church shooting, I could have said, "Oh, that's really sad." I could have felt bad for a few minutes and then returned to my own disappointments. But I refused to do that, because I am not going to live with that kind of attitude. After I heard about the crisis, I thought for a few minutes and decided to ask my son to call the pastor and find out what we could do to help them. Maybe the families who lost loved ones need something or perhaps just knowing someone cares will help.

I am amazed when I think of how often we go through hard times and no one even calls. I believe people think everyone is doing it, so nobody does it.

Whose Job Is It?

This is a story I heard years ago about four people named Everybody, Somebody, Anybody, and Nobody. There was an important job to be done and Everybody was sure Somebody would do it. Anybody could have done it, but Nobody did it. Somebody got angry about that because it was Everybody's job. Everybody thought Anybody could do it, but Nobody realized that Everybody wouldn't do it. In the end, Everybody blamed Somebody when Nobody did what Anybody could have done.

I once read about a shocking incident that shows the principles of this story at work—tragically—in real life. In 1964 Catherine Genovese was stabbed to death over a period of thirty-five minutes while thirty-eight neighbors watched. Their reaction was described as cold and uncaring, a result of urban apathy and alienation. Later, research by Latane and Darley revealed that no one had helped simply because there were so many observers. The observers looked to one another for guidance on what to do. Since no one was doing anything, they determined that no one should be doing anything.

People are less likely to receive help in time of need as the number of bystanders increases. A student appearing to have an epileptic seizure was helped 85 percent of the time when only one bystander was present, but when several people were standing by and watching he received help only 31 percent of the time.

This study proves that the more people do nothing, the more people will do nothing, but if even a small group of committed people will begin to reach out to others with care and love, smiles and compliments, appreciation and respect, etc., the movement can and will grow.

Studies have proven that we are very affected by what people around us do. We look to one another for direction even when we are totally unaware that we are doing it. Most people will agree with the majority even if they really don't agree. They do it just to remain part of the group.

If we want to be part of the Love Revolution, we as Christians must become the example to others instead of merely melting into the world's system. Had someone simply been bold enough to take action or loving enough to help, Catherine Genovese's life might have been spared.

Are You Praying Prayers God Can Answer?

I would like to suggest something for you to add to your daily prayers. Each day ask God what you can do for Him. Then as you go through your day, watch for opportunities to do what you believe Jesus would do if He were still on Earth in bodily form. He lives in you now if you are a Christian and you are His ambassador, so make sure you represent Him well. I spent lots of years in my morning prayers telling the Lord what I needed Him to do for me, but only lately have I added this new part: "God, what can I do for You today?"

Recently, I was asking God to help a friend who was going through a very difficult time. She needed something, so I asked God to provide it. To my surprise, His answer to me was, "Stop asking Me to meet the need; ask Me to show you what *you* can do." I have become aware that I often ask God to do things for me when He wants me to do those things myself. He doesn't expect me to do anything without His help, but neither will He do everything for me while I sit idly by. God wants us to be open to being involved. He wants us to use our resources to help people, and if what we have isn't enough to meet their

> God wants us to be open to being involved.

needs, then we can encourage others to get involved so that together we can do what needs to be done.

I encourage you to pray prayers God can answer. You and He are partners, and He wants to work *with* and *through* you. Ask Him to show you what you can do, and depend on Him to give you not only the creativity, but the resources to do it.

Don't panic when I say, "Use your resources." I am talking about more than money. Our resources include our energy, time, talents, and material possessions, as well as our finances. Helping someone may involve money, but it often involves time, and I think we are so strapped for time in our society that we often find it easier to write a check than to take the time to care about the individual who has the need. I have come to believe that what I call the ministry of "being there" is often what people need most.

A friend of mine lives in a large city where homelessness is a huge problem. One winter night she was coming home from work and walked by a man asking for money. It was cold and dark, she'd put in a long day and she was anxious to get home. Not wanting to pull out her wallet in a less than safe situation, she reached deep into her purse fishing for change. As her fingers searched in vain, the man started telling her that his coat had been stolen in the homeless shelter where he'd stayed the night before and described a few other troubles he was having. Still trying to come up with a couple of quarters, she nodded at the right times and said "that's too bad" now and then. When she finally found the money, she dropped it into the man's cup. He smiled and said, "Thank you for talking with me." My friend says she realized that night that the fifty cents she gave him was appreciated, but what meant the most to that man was the fact that someone had heard what he said and responded.

We have a team of people from our ministry who try to help people living in the tunnels under the downtown bridge. They have found that each of these people had a life prior to the tunnels and they all have story. Something tragic happened to them that resulted in them being in their present circumstance. They appreciate the sandwiches and the rides to church where they can shower and get clean clothes, but mostly they appreciate someone caring enough to actually talk with them long enough to find who they are and what has happened to them.

Let me encourage you to do everything you can to help others. If they simply need you to be there, then take time to do so. Ask God what He wants you do to—and He will answer your prayer so you can do it.

Practice Aggressive Goodness

Do you believe the world is filled with injustice? Do you think something should be done about starving children? Should somebody help the 1.1 million people who have no safe drinking water? Should people live on streets and under bridges? Should a family you have gone to church with for years experience a tragedy and not even get a phone call from anyone to find out why they have not been in church for three months? If a church of another denomination in your city burns down, is it proper to just pray and do nothing practical to help? Do you believe somebody should do something about injustice? I somehow think you have answered all of these questions correctly, so I have one final question. What are you going to do? Will you be the "somebody" who does what needs to be done?

When I ask what you are going to do, do you perhaps feel fear because you wonder what "doing something" will require? I understand that kind of panicky feeling. After all, if I really decide to forget myself and start aggressively trying to help, what will happen to me? Who will take care of me if I don't take care of myself? God said He would, so I think we should find out if He really meant what He said. Why not retire from "self care," and see if God can do a better job than you have done. If we take care of His business, which is helping hurting people, I believe He will take care of ours.

Just Keep Moving

As I close this chapter, let me say that I realize things happen in life that cause us to want to retreat from the world for a while. I realize that major life changes occur and require a period of readjustment, and I realize that loss or trauma can make people not want to interact with or reach out to others. I am sympathetic to these things, and if you have experienced a loss of some kind and it has left you numb and not feeling like doing anything, I understand how you feel, but I want to encourage you to force yourself to keep moving. Satan wants to isolate you because you may not have the strength to defeat his lies by yourself. I know that it may sound almost ridiculous to tell you to go help somebody else, but I believe with all my heart that doing so is a protection for you as well as the answer to the world's problems.

Let me say it again: I firmly believe we need a Love Revolution. We've all tried selfishness and depression, discouragement, and self-pity—and we have seen the fruit of that. The world is filled with the results of these things. Let's join together in agreement that we will live life God's way. Be mindful to be a blessing to others (see Gal. 6:10). Put on love (see Col. 3:14). That means to be active on purpose in reaching out to others. Watch and pray for opportunities; be a spy for God! Jesus got up daily and went about doing good (see Acts 10:38). It seems so simple. I wonder how we have missed it all this time.

CHAPTER
4

Interrupted by God

Now is the accepted time, not tomorrow, not some more
convenient season. It is today that our best work can be
done and not some future day or future year.

W.E.B. DuBois

I frequently stay in hotels during my ministry travels, and when
I am in my room I always put the "Do Not Disturb" sign on the
door so nobody will bother me. Putting such a sign on my hotel
room door is acceptable, but having one on my life is not.

Have you ever noticed that God does not always do things on
your timetable or in ways that are convenient? Paul told Timothy that as a servant of God and a minister of the gospel, he had
to fulfill his duties whether it was convenient or inconvenient
(see 2 Tim. 4:2). I doubt Timothy was nearly as addicted to convenience as we are today, yet Paul thought it was important to
remind him to be prepared to be inconvenienced or interrupted
by God. If Timothy needed to hear that, I am sure we also need

to hear it frequently, because we are probably more attached to convenience than Timothy was. All I have to do to recognize how much I value convenience is listen to myself complain when even the smallest device I have doesn't work properly—the dishwasher, air conditioner, hair dryer, clothes dryer, washing machine, microwave, or countless other things.

I watch people in our conferences in America complain because they have to park a few blocks away from the conference venue, yet in India people walk three days to get to a Bible conference. I watch people in America disturb those around them to go to the bathroom or get a drink of water or take a phone call, but in India people sit in the dirt for literally most of the day without ever considering getting up. In my country, they complain if it is too cold or too hot, yet when I go to India the only people I hear complaining about the heat are the ones I brought with me, including myself.

I do believe we have an addiction to convenience. I'm not suggesting that we unplug our modern conveniences, and I certainly understand that we desire what we are accustomed to, but we do need to have the proper mind-set about convenience. If we can have it, thank God (literally). But not being able to have it should never stop us from doing anything God asks us to do.

I recall a time several years ago when a blind couple wanted to come to our Wednesday night teaching sessions, which were held at a banquet center in St. Louis. They normally took the bus, but their usual route was canceled, so the only way they could continue coming would be for someone to pick them up and take them home. What an opportunity! I thought people would be standing in line to help, but nobody was willing to do it because they lived in an area considered "out of the way."

In other words, providing transportation for this couple would have been inconvenient. I remember having to get one of our employees to do it, which meant we had to pay that person. It is amazing how much more willing we are to "help" if we are going to get money for it. We must remember that the love of money is the root of all evil. We cannot allow money to be our main motivator in life. We all need money, but we also need to do things for other people, and the fact that these acts of kindness are inconvenient sometimes is actually good for us. Often, such opportunities are "testing times," times when God checks to see whether or not we are committed. If you are willing to do something kind for someone else with no pay and perhaps no credit, it is a positive sign that your spiritual heart is in good condition.

When God wanted to see if the Israelites would obey His commands, He led them the long, hard way in the wilderness (see Deut. 8:1–2). Sometimes He does the same with us. We are very willing to "obey" God when it is easy and we are being quickly rewarded for our efforts. But what about when it is inconvenient, when it is not according to our plan, and when there seems to be nothing in it for us? How obedient are we then? These are questions we all need to ask ourselves because it's very important to be honest about our commitment. It is easy to stand in church and sing "I Surrender All," but what do we do when the surrender is more than a song and is actually a requirement?

God, This Is Just Not a Good Time

The Bible tells a story about a man who did not follow God because doing so would have been inconvenient. This man, named Felix, asked Paul to come and preach the gospel to him. But when Paul started talking to him about right living, purity of life, and control of the passions, Felix became alarmed and frightened. He told Paul to go away and that he would call him at a more convenient time (see Acts 24:25). I find this extremely amusing, not because it is really funny, but because it clearly depicts the way we are. We don't mind hearing about how much God loves us and about the good plans He has for our lives, but when He begins to chastise us or correct us in any way, we try to tell Him that "now" is just not a good time. I doubt He ever chooses a time we would consider, "a good time," and I think He does that on purpose!

When the Israelites were traveling through the wilderness, they were led by a cloud during the day and a pillar of fire by night. When the cloud moved, they had to move and when it hovered, they stayed where they were. The interesting thing is that there was no pattern or plan they knew of concerning when the cloud might move. They simply had to move when the cloud did (see Num. 9:15–23). The Bible says that sometimes it moved during the day and sometimes it moved at night. Sometimes it rested for a few days and sometimes it rested for one day. I seriously doubt that at night they all hung "Do Not Disturb" signs on the openings of their tents to let God know they did not want to be inconvenienced. When He decided it was time to make progress they packed up and followed Him, and when He decides it is time for us to move to the next level of our journey in Him, we should never say, "This is just not a good time!"

Wouldn't it have been nice if God had provided a monthly calendar showing all the moving days so they could have been mentally, emotionally, and physically prepared? I wonder why He didn't do that. Was it simply because He interrupts us on purpose just to see how we will respond?

God knows best and His timing is always exactly right. The fact that I don't *feel* ready to deal with something in my life doesn't mean that I'm not ready. God is the head of the "ways and means" committee. His ways are not our ways, but they are higher and better than our ways (see Isa. 55:9).

Why Isn't It Easier?

If God wants us to help people, why doesn't He make it easy and cost effective? Let me answer that question with another question. Did Jesus sacrifice anything to purchase our freedom from sin and bondage? I wonder why God didn't make the plan of salvation easier. After all, He could have devised any plan He wanted to and simply said, "This is going to work." It seems that in God's economy nothing cheap is worth having. King David said he would not give God that which cost him nothing (see 2 Sam. 24:24). I have learned that true giving is not giving until I can feel it. Giving away all my clothes and household items that are old and I am finished with may be a nice gesture, but it does not equate to real giving. Real giving occurs when I give somebody something that I want to keep. I am sure you have had those testing times when God asks you to give away something that you like. He gave us His only Son because He loves us, so what will love cause us to do? Can we at least be inconvenienced or uncomfortable occasionally in order to help someone in need?

I recently saw a story on television about a young couple who were very much in love and were soon to be married. Tragically, she was in a car accident that left her in a coma for months. The man she was to marry sat by her side day after day and finally she woke up, but she had brain damage and would forever be crippled and unable to do many things for herself. The young man did not even consider not going ahead with the wedding. She went down the aisle in a wheelchair, not being able to speak clearly due to her injuries but obviously extremely joyful. For the remainder of his life the young man cared for her and they enjoyed life together. With his help and encouragement she even became part of the Special Olympics and was able to accomplish amazing things.

It would have been so easy and even understandable to most of us if the young man had simply walked away. After all, staying with her meant that he would be inconvenienced and need to sacrifice daily. However, he did not walk away as so many do when faced with situations that will be uncomfortable for them. He stayed and in all probability experienced more joy in life than most of us do.

If you are like me, you really enjoy reading about people who sacrificed so much for the benefit of others, but I suspect that God wants you and me to do more than read their stories. Perhaps He wants you to have a story of your own.

Inconvenienced for Someone Else's Convenience

God will interrupt one person and ask him or her to do something inconvenient in order to make life more convenient for another person. We must understand God's ways or we will resist what we should embrace. The simple truth is this: We must give in order to be happy, and giving is not true giving if we don't feel the sacrifice of it.

Peter, Andrew, James, John, and the other disciples were greatly honored. They were chosen to be the twelve disciples, the men who would learn from Jesus and then carry the gospel to the world. They were all busy when Jesus called them. They had lives, families, and businesses to take care of. With no warning at all, Jesus showed up and said, "Follow Me." The Bible says Peter and Andrew were casting their nets into the sea when Jesus called them, and they left their nets and followed Him (see Matt. 4:18–21). Talk about an interruption! He did not tell them they could pray about it, or consider it, or go home and talk to their wives and children. He merely said, "Follow Me."

They didn't ask how long they would be gone or what the salary package would be. They didn't ask about benefits, compensation time for travel, or what kind of hotel they would be staying in. They didn't even ask Him what their job description would be. They simply left all and followed Him. Even when I read about this now, I must admit it seems a bit severe, but perhaps the greater the opportunity is, the greater the sacrifice must be.

I remember a time when I was complaining about some of the things God seemed to be requiring of me, because I felt others didn't have the same requirements placed on them. He simply said, "Joyce, you have asked Me for a lot. Do you want it or not?" I had asked to be able to help people all over the world, and I was learning that the privilege of doing so would frequently be inconvenient and uncomfortable.

It is impossible to have a harvest without sowing seed. King Solomon said that if we wait for all conditions to be favorable before we sow, we will never reap (see Eccles. 11:4). In other words, we must give and obey God when it is not convenient and when it is costly. Perhaps these twelve men were the ones chosen because they were willing to do what others were not willing to do. Although the Bible does not say Jesus called any who refused Him, perhaps He did. Perhaps He had to speak to thousands to get the twelve. At least I think that's the way it is today. People who are willing to sacrifice, to be inconvenienced, and to have their plans interrupted are few. Many sing of their love for Jesus and that is nice, but we must also remember that although singing is fun, it does not require sacrifice. Real love requires sacrifice.

I believe that there is not much real love displayed in the world because it takes effort and always costs something. We need to remember this reality if we are seriously going to participate in a Love Revolution. It is always wise to count the cost before making any kind of commitment, otherwise we probably won't finish what we start.

Interrupted by God

The more I study the men and women in the Bible who we consider to be "great," the more I see that they all made huge sacrifices and there was nothing convenient about what God asked them to do.

Abraham had to leave his country, his relatives, and his home and go to a place God would not even tell him about until he went there. Perhaps he thought he might end up in a palace as a king or something, but instead he wandered from place to place, living in temporary tents. He ended up in Egypt—a land that was "oppressive (intense and grievous)"—in the midst of a famine (Gen. 12:10). Although the sacrifice was great, Abraham was given the privilege of being the man with whom God made a covenant agreement, and through him all families of the earth have the opportunity to be blessed by God (see Gen. 22:18). *Wow!*

Joseph saved a nation from starvation, but not before God violently removed him from his comfortable home where he was Daddy's favorite and put him in an inconvenient place for many years. God did that in order to position Joseph to be in the right place at the right time. But Joseph could only know that after the fact. We often don't understand why we are where we are, and say, "God, what am I doing here?" I know I have said that to God many times, and although He didn't bother to answer me at the time, I can look back now and realize that each place where I was became part of where I am today.

Esther saved the Jews from destruction, but God certainly interrupted her plan in order for her to do so. She was a young maiden who without doubt had plans for her future when suddenly, without warning, she was asked to enter the king's harem and gain favor with him so she could reveal the plan of wicked Haman, who intended to slaughter the Jews.

She was asked to do things that left her frightened for her life, but her uncle wisely said: "For if you keep silent at this time, relief and deliverance shall arise for the Jews from elsewhere, but you and your father's house will perish. And who knows but that you have come to the kingdom for such a time as this and for this very occasion?" (Esther 4:14).

Had she not made the sacrifice, God would have found someone else, but saving her people was her destiny. It was her purpose in life. Don't miss your purpose in life just because you don't want God to interrupt your plans.

The list of people who entered into sacrificial obedience

could go on and on. The Bible calls them men "of whom the world was not worthy" (Heb. 11:38).

These people we read about were inconvenienced so that someone else's life could be easier. Jesus died so we could have life and have it abundantly. Soldiers die so that civilians can remain safe at home. Fathers go to work so their families can have nice lives and mothers go through the pain of childbirth to bring another life into the world. It seems quite obvious that someone usually has to experience pain or inconvenience for anyone to gain anything.

This chapter is very important because if being part of a Love Revolution is merely an idea that gives you a nice feeling, you will change your mind about being part of it when you realize that you will need to do some things you would rather not do in order to walk in love. You may have to put up with someone you would rather get away from because love bears with the failings and weaknesses of others. You might have to stay in a place that is not much fun simply because you are the only light in the darkness. You might have to leave a place because the surroundings are tempting you to sin. Actually, Abraham was living in the midst of idol worshippers including his family, so it is no wonder God asked him to get away from the place and the people. Sometimes God must separate us from what we are familiar with in order to show us what He wants us to see.

If you will make the decision that you don't mind inconvenience or interruption, then God can use you. You can make a

> If you will make the decision that you don't mind inconvenience or interruption, then God can use you.

difference in the world. But if you remain addicted to your own comfort, God will have to pass you by for someone with a stronger stomach for the hard things in life.

Sodom and Gomorrah

You have probably heard of Sodom and Gomorrah and the terrible wickedness in those cities. But what did they actually do that was so displeasing to God? We often have the idea that their sexual perversion finally put God over the edge and caused Him to destroy them, but it was actually quite a different situation that caused Him to act against them. I was shocked when I saw the truth behind their destruction. I discovered it while searching Scriptures about the need to feed the poor. "Behold, *this was the iniquity* of your sister Sodom: pride, overabundance of food, prosperous ease, and idleness were hers and her daughters'; neither did she strengthen the hand of the poor and the needy. And they were haughty and committed abominable offenses before Me; therefore I removed them when I saw it and I saw fit" (Ezek. 16:49–50, emphasis mine).

The problem with Sodom and Gomorrah was that they had too much and were not sharing it with those in need. They were idle and lived excessively convenient lifestyles, which led them to commit abominable acts. We see clearly from this that idleness and too much convenience is not good for us and leads us into more and more trouble. Failing to share what we do have with those who have less than we do is not good for us and is actually dangerous because this selfish type of lifestyle opens the door for evil to progress. Not only are these things not good for us, but they are offensive to God. He expects us to be channels for Him to flow through, not reservoirs that hold everything we have for ourselves.

We appreciate all the conveniences that are available to us today, but in some ways I think Satan is using them to destroy any willingness to be inconvenienced in order to obey God or help others in need. We have become addicted to ease and we need to be very careful. Like most people, I like nice, comfortable things. I like convenience, but I have also made an effort not to complain when I don't have things the way I want them. I also realize that inconvenience is almost always part of helping others and I know I am called by God to help people and do so with a good attitude.

I don't like to be interrupted while I am writing. It is very inconvenient for me if I am interrupted because then I have to work to get back in the flow of what I was working on. Just a few moments ago I was tested. My phone rang and I saw it was a woman that I knew would need me to listen to her for probably quite some time about her troubled marriage. I didn't necessarily want to stop but I felt that I should because this particular woman is a well-known person who has nobody she can trust to talk to. Just because a person is well known to the world does not mean they are not lonely. She is a lonely, internationally known woman with a problem and God wanted me to interrupt my writing on love to actually practice it!! Imagine that...God wants us to practice what we say we believe.

CHAPTER
5

Love Finds a Way

Failure will never overtake me if my
determination to succeed is strong enough.
Og Mandino

Desire is a powerful motivator. I have finally faced the truth
that if I genuinely want to do something, I will find a way to
do it. People frequently ask me how I do everything I do, and I
simply say, "Because I want to." I realize that God has given me
grace and put desires in my heart, but it is the fact that I *want*
to do certain things that motivates me to do them. I want to do
what God wants me to do; I want to help people and I want to
fulfill my destiny, or as the apostle Paul said, "I want to finish
my race."

You might ask, "What if I don't have that desire?" You obviously do have a desire to do God's will or you would have put
this book down after you read the first chapter. If you have a relationship with God through Jesus Christ, then you have a desire

to do good because He has given you His heart and Spirit. Ezekiel 11:19 promises this: "And I will give them one heart [a new heart] and I will put a new spirit within them; and I will take the stony [unnaturally hardened] heart out of their flesh, and will give them a heart of flesh [sensitive and responsive to the touch of their God]." We may become lazy, passive, or selfish and need to deal with those issues at times, but as believers it is impossible to have the heart of God and not want to obey Him and help people.

I guess the question is: How much do you want it? Do you want to do His will more than you want to do your will? Do you want it enough to sacrifice others things to have it?

I recently had a young man tell me how unhappy he was. He went on to tell me that he knew God was calling him to come to a higher place but he felt that he was not willing to make the sacrifice needed. I felt sad for him because I don't want him to miss the joy that is on the other side of sacrifice. I pray he will change his mind.

If we really want to do something, we'll find a way to do it. Unless we admit this, we will spend our lives deceived by our own excuses about why we cannot do things. Excuses are very dangerous, and I believe they are one of the main reasons we don't make the progress we desire. Perhaps you would like to exercise, but you make an excuse about why you can't. Maybe you want to spend more time with your family, but you have an excuse about why you just can't. You might realize you need to give more of yourself to help others and you may want to do it, but there are always reasons (excuses) why you don't actually do it. Satan is the one who gives us excuses; until we realize that excuses are keeping us deceived and disobedient, we will be stuck in joyless, fruitless living.

A Good Neighbor

Jesus said, "You must love the Lord your God with all your heart and with all your soul and with all your strength and with all your mind; and your neighbor as yourself" (Luke 10:27). He went on to say to the lawyer to whom He was speaking that if he would do so, he would live, which meant he would enjoy active, blessed, endless life in the kingdom of God. Wanting to acquit himself of any reproach, the lawyer said, "And who is my neighbor?" He wanted to know exactly who these people were that he was supposed to be showing love to, and Jesus responded by telling him a story.

A man who was traveling was attacked by robbers who took his belongings and beat him, then left him half dead, lying on the side of the road. Along came a priest (a religious man) who saw the man needing help and he passed by on the other side of the road. I don't know if he was already on the other side of the road or if he crossed the road so the injured man could not even see him and perhaps ask for help, but he made sure he did not have to walk by the hurting man. Then another religious man, a Levite, came along who also passed by on the other side of the road. Perhaps these religious men were hurrying to get to church and had no time to actually do what the church should have been teaching them to do. Religious people often respond to need with religious words but with no offer of practical help. I believe this is one of biggest problems we have today in Christianity. We are proud of what we supposedly "know," but in many cases we are not doing much with the knowledge we have. We talk a lot, but we don't always show people what they need to see—and that is love in action.

After these two religious men passed by the man who desperately needed help, a Samaritan man, not a particularly religious man, traveled the road. When he noticed the needy man he was moved with pity and sympathy and went to him and dressed his wounds. After that, he put him on his own horse and took him to a local inn and gave the innkeeper two days' wages and told him to take care of the man until he returned, at which time he would pay him for additional expenses. Jesus then asked the lawyer which of the three men proved himself to be a neighbor (see Luke 10:27–37).

Several aspects of this story catch my attention. First, as I've already mentioned, the religious men did nothing. We must refuse to do nothing! Even if what we can do is small, we absolutely must find a way to do something when it comes to meeting the needs God makes us aware of. I admit there are times when all we can do is pray or perhaps offer some verbal encouragement, but we should at least be aggressive enough to look for a way to help. We should at least think about it and not just assume we can do nothing or, even worse, find an excuse to do nothing simply because we don't want to be bothered.

The next thing that strikes me in this story is that the Samaritan went to quite a bit of trouble to help the man. I imagine that delayed his journey significantly. He was obviously going somewhere he needed to go because he left the injured man long enough to go take care of his business before he returned. He made an investment of time and money, and he was willing to be inconvenienced in order to take care of someone in need.

I also see that the Samaritan did not let an emergency need distract him from his original purpose. This is also important because sometimes people are so driven by the emotions of compassion that they cannot stay focused on their goals long enough to accomplish them. Our daughter Sandra loves, loves, loves to help people and that is a good thing, but just yesterday she called and asked me to pray for her to have balance and clarity about whom to help and to what degree. She has twin daughters to care for, she teaches a parenting class at her church, and she also has some other commitments she feels she needs to be faithful to and yet she keeps hearing about needs and always wants to help! Quite often she gets involved in helping without even thinking through what it will mean or how she can help without ignoring her other priorities. The result is that sometimes in her good desire to help she ends up frustrated and feeling confused, which is not God's will at all.

I encouraged Sandra to do what the Samaritan did in Jesus' story, and I would encourage you likewise. Be willing to change your plan and be inconvenienced, and be willing to give some time and money if necessary to help meet the need. But don't try to do everything yourself when there are others who can help too. The Samaritan enlisted the innkeeper to help him meet the need so he could remain focused on whatever it was he was on his way to do.

The devil doesn't seem to mind which ditch we are in as long as we are not in the middle of the road. In other words, people either don't do anything or they try to do it all and then become discouraged or eventually feel they are being taken advantage of. Every aspect of our lives requires balance, even the area of helping others. I have learned the hard way that I cannot do everything and do anything well, and this is true for all of us. But, I cannot let a fear of getting too involved keep me from being involved at all.

I also see that the Samaritan did not put limits on what he was willing to allow this need to cost him. He told the innkeeper he would give him whatever it cost to care for the injured man when he returned. Rarely do we find anyone who is willing to do *whatever* needs to be done.

As I said, sometimes we must place limits in order to protect our other priorities, but in this case the man apparently had plenty of money, so he had no need to put limits on it. He acted out of a generous attitude, not a fearful one. God may not ask any one of us to do everything required to solve a problem or meet a need, but He does want each of us to do what we can. And, if He should ask us to do it all then we should do it all! Giving our all is challenging and it stretches our faith to new levels but it also brings the freedom of knowing that nothing in this world has a hold on us.

I remember a time when God asked me to give everything I had saved of my personal money including all gift certificates. This new level of sacrificing *all* was hard because I had been saving the money a long time and had plans to go shopping at the right time. Oddly enough, the gift certificates were the most difficult. I had several very nice ones that I had received for my birthday and I enjoyed just knowing they were available should I want to use them. I was accustomed to giving, but giving *all* was a new level. After some time of arguing with God and making every excuse I could think of, I finally obeyed. The pain of letting go of the possessions was momentary, but the joy of obedience and the knowledge that possessions had no hold on me was everlasting.

That was the first time I was tested in that way, but it has not been the last. God chooses the time for testing and it is necessary for our benefit. It keeps us from getting too attached to things. God wants us to enjoy what He gives us, but He also wants us to remember that we are stewards, not owners. He is the Master and our job is to serve Him with joy with our whole heart and every resource we have.

Who Is My Neighbor?

Who should you help and who is your neighbor? It is whoever happens to be in your path with a need. It may be someone who needs you to listen, or perhaps someone who needs a compliment or encouragement. It could be someone who needs a little of your time or perhaps someone for whom you can meet or help meet a financial need. Maybe your neighbor is someone who feels lonely and just needs you to be friendly.

Dave recently told me that God had dealt with him about taking time to be friendly. I've always thought he's very friendly, but he feels that God wants him to put even more time into it. He asks people all kinds of things about themselves to show that he cares about them as individuals. Many of the people he spends time with he does not know at all and will probably never see again. Sometimes they are elderly or people from another country who don't speak English very well and might feel a bit out of place. He recently told me about a handicapped man others were staring at in a coffee shop. Dave took the time to talk with the gentleman, even though his handicap made understanding his speech difficult.

We often avoid people who are different than we are in some way because they make us feel uncomfortable or incapable.

Perhaps we should think more about how they feel rather than doing what is convenient for us.

The list of ways we can show ourselves to be good neighbors is probably endless, but if we really want to help people and be a blessing we will find a way. Remember, indifference makes an excuse, but love finds a way.

Little Things with a Big Impact

Jesus did not waste His time, so we can assume that everything He did was very meaningful and contains a great lesson to be learned. Let's think about the time He decided to wash His disciples' feet (see John 13:1–17). What was that all about? He had in mind several lessons He wanted to teach the disciples, one of which was the need to serve one another. Jesus was and is the Son of God. Actually, He is God manifested in the second person of the Trinity. So it suffices to say that He is really important and certainly would not have to wash anyone's feet, especially not guys who were His students. But He did so because He wanted to teach them that they could be in authority and still be servants at the same time. Many today have failed to learn that important lesson.

In Jesus' day, people's feet were fairly dirty. People traveled on dirt roads and wore shoes that amounted to a few straps with a sole. The custom of the day was to wash the feet of guests when they entered a home, but servants typically performed that duty, not the master of the house. Jesus actually took off His garment and put on a servant's towel. This was another gesture intended to teach a lesson. He wanted to show that we can lay aside our "positions" in life long enough to serve someone else and not be fearful of losing them.

Peter, the most vocal disciple, vehemently refused to let Jesus wash his feet, but Jesus said that if He did not wash Peter's feet, the two of them could not be real friends. In other words, they had to be doing things for one another in order for their relationship to be healthy and strong. How many marriages could be saved or at least greatly improved if couples applied this principle?

I decided a few years ago that I was not willing to have any more one-sided relationships—relationships in which I do all the giving and the other person does all the taking. That kind of interaction is not real relationship, and it always eventually causes resentment and bitterness. Not only should we do things for each other, we actually *need* to do things for one another. This is part of maintaining good relationships.

> Not only should we do things for each other, we actually *need* to do things for one another.

We do a lot for our children, but they also do things for us. What they do may be something we could easily do ourselves, but they need to give to us as well as receive from us, and we need them to do so.

Giving does not always have to be a response to a desperate need. We may be led to do something for people who don't seem to need what we can do for them at all. If there is no need, then why do it? Simply because giving of any kind encourages people and makes them feel loved, and we all need to feel loved, no matter how many "things" we have. Use the resources you have to be a blessing and you will never run out of resources.

Washing feet was a menial task reserved for servants, but it contained a great lesson: Humble yourself and be willing to do small things that may have a huge impact.

Little Things Mean a Lot

We took the band Delirious? to India with us on a mission trip, and Stu, their drummer at the time, was given a little strip of leather from a poor girl who wore it as a bracelet. The small gesture of love from one who had so little was life changing for Stu. He has said publicly that as long as he lives, he will never forget the lesson it taught him. If someone with so little was willing to give, what could he be doing? Yes, little things can have a huge impact.

What little thing could you do? Jesus washed feet and said we would be blessed and happy if we would follow His example. Below is a partial list of some things the Bible says we can and should do for one another:

- Watch over one another
- Pray for one another
- Be mindful to be a blessing
- Look for kindnesses we can express to others
- Be friendly and hospitable
- Be patient with one another
- Bear with others' faults and weaknesses
- Give others the benefit of the doubt

- Forgive one another
- Comfort one another
- Be faithful
- Be loyal
- Build up one another—encourage others, reminding them of their strengths when they feel weak
- Be happy for people when they are blessed
- Prefer one another (let someone go ahead of us or give them the best of something)
- Consider one another
- Keep people's secrets and don't tell their faults
- Believe the best of one another

As I said, this is a partial list. Love has many faces or many ways it can be seen. We will discuss several of them as the book continues. The ideas I listed here are relatively simple things we all can do if we are willing. We don't have to make special plans for most of them, but can do them throughout the day as we encounter opportunities.

> So then, as occasion and opportunity open up to us,
> let us do good [morally] to all people...
> *Galatians 6:10*

Love Must Express Itself

We often think of love as a thing, but the word love is also a verb. Love must do something in order to remain what it is. Part of the nature of love is that it requires expression. The Bible asks if we see a need and close our heart of compassion how can the love of God live and remain in us (see 1 John 3:17). Love becomes weaker and weaker if it cannot be demonstrated; in fact, it may become totally inactive. If we remain active on purpose as we do things for others, we can keep from being selfish, idle, and unfruitful. The quintessential act of love is that Jesus laid down His own life for us. And we ought to lay down our lives for one another. That sounds extreme, doesn't it? Fortunately, the great majority of us will never be called upon to give up our physical life for someone else. But we have opportunities every day to "lay down" our life for another. Every time you put aside your own desire or need and replace it with an act of love for someone else, you are laying down your life for a moment, or an hour, or a day.

If we are full of the love of God, and we are because the Holy Spirit fills our hearts with love at the new birth, then we must let love flow out of us. If it becomes stagnant through inactivity, it is good for nothing. God so loved the world that He gave His only Son (see John 3:16). Do you get it? God's love provoked Him to give! It is useless to say we love people if we do nothing for them. Put a huge sign in your house, perhaps in several places, that asks, "What have I done to help someone today?" This will serve to remind you of your goal while you are developing new habits and becoming a love revolutionary.

Love is all about action. It is not a theory or merely words. Words are important and we can actually use our words as one method of loving people, but we should use all means possible to keep on showing love among ourselves.

What can you do to show love to someone today? Take the time to think about it and make a plan. Don't go through the day without increasing someone else's joy.

CHAPTER
6

Overcome Evil with Good

All that is necessary for the triumph of
evil is for good men to do nothing.
Edmund Burke

Doing nothing is easy, but it is also very dangerous. For where there is no opposition to evil, it multiplies. We all fall often into the trap of complaining about the things that are wrong in our society and in life, but complaining does nothing except discourage us even more. It changes nothing, because there is no positive power in it.

Imagine what a mess the world would be if all God did was complain about everything that has gone wrong since He created it. But God doesn't complain. He just continues to be good and work for justice. He knows He can overcome evil with good! Evil is powerful for sure, but good is more powerful.

We need to stop and realize that God works through His people. Yes, God is good all the time. But He has chosen to work

on this earth through His children—you and me. It's humbling
to realize that He could do so much more if we would be committed to love and do good at all times. We need to remember Jesus' instruction in Matthew 5:16: "Let your light so shine
before men that they may see your moral excellence and your
praiseworthy, noble, and good deeds and recognize and honor
and praise and glorify your Father Who is in heaven."

Goodness Is Powerful

The more we respond to evil with evil, the more it increases.
I am reminded of a movie entitled *El Cid*, the story of the man
who united Spain and became a great hero using the principle I
am talking about. For centuries, the Christians had fought with
the Moors. They hated and killed each other. In battle, El Cid
captured five Moors, but refused to kill them because he realized that the killing had never done any good. He believed that
showing mercy to his enemies would change their hearts, and
then both groups could live in peace. Although he was initially
labeled a traitor for his actions, they eventually proved to work
and he was honored as a hero.

One of the Moors he captured said, "Anyone can kill, but
only a true king can show mercy to his enemies." Because of his
one act of kindness, El Cid's enemies offered themselves to him
as friends and allies from that point on. Jesus is a true king and
He is good, kind, and merciful to all. Can we do any less than
follow His example?

Right now, can you think of anyone to whom you could show
mercy? Is there someone who has treated you wrongly that you

can be good to? Being merciful and good, especially to your enemies, may be one of the most powerful things you have ever done.

Prayer Works

In the past several years, we have seen evil progress rapidly through the wicked things shown on television and portrayed in movies. I was appalled years ago when psychics began to have programs on television. They offered to tell people their futures for a fee. Anyone who was willing to pay several dollars per minute could call in and get a so-called "reading." I frequently complained about this, making comments such as, "I just think it is terrible that they are allowing things like this on television. So many people are just wasting their money and they are being deceived." I heard many others saying basically the same thing. One day God dropped this thought into my heart, *If you and everyone else who complains had spent that time praying about the psychics, I could have already done something about it.* I began to pray and ask several others to do the same. Before long most, if not all, of those types of programs were exposed as fraudulent and taken off the air.

We often tend to complain about what "they" are doing, as I did when "they" began to air psychic television broadcasts, yet we do nothing to make the situation better. Prayer is a good thing that does have the power to overcome evil, so we should pray about anything we are tempted to complain about. God considers complaining and murmuring evil, but faith-filled prayers are powerful and effective. Praying opens the door for God to work and do something good.

Respond Properly to Evil

While trying to make their journey through the wilderness to get to the Promised Land, the Israelites encountered trials and difficulties and responded by complaining, grumbling, and murmuring about all of them. They indulged in immorality of all kinds and one of their sins was complaining. It allowed the destroyer access to their lives and many of them died (see 1 Cor. 10:8–11). Had they responded to their trials by remaining thankful to God, worshipping and praising Him, and being good to one another, I believe they would have made it through the wilderness in much less time. Instead, most of them fell by the wayside in the desert and never reached their destination. I wonder how many times we never see the good results we desire simply because we respond to evil things that happen with complaints instead of prayer, praise, thanksgiving, and continuing to reach out to other people in need.

Faith and Love

For many, many years a large portion of the teaching I heard in church and conferences was about faith, and the books I read were about faith. It seemed the main topic of teaching throughout the Christian world was, "Trust God and everything will be all right."

Without faith we cannot please God (see Heb. 11:6), so we definitely need to put our faith in Him and trust Him, but there's something else in God's Word that I believe completes the picture we need to see. I will share it with you, but first let me tell you about some of my experiences in the early years of my journey with God.

I received Jesus as my Savior at the age of nine, but didn't understand what I had in Him or how a relationship with Him could change my life because I had no "continuing education" in spiritual matters. The home I grew up in was dysfunctional, to say the least. My father was an alcoholic, unfaithful to my mother with numerous women, and he was very violent and angry. As I mentioned earlier, he also abused me sexually on a regular basis. The list goes on and on, but I am sure you get the picture.

Now, fast forward to my life at the age of twenty-three. I married Dave and started going to church with him. I loved God and wanted to learn, so I took classes that eventually allowed me to be confirmed in the denomination and went to church regularly. I did learn about God's love and grace, as well as learning many church doctrines that were important to the foundation of my faith.

At the age of thirty-two, I found myself very frustrated because my Christianity didn't seem to be helping me in my practical, everyday life. I believed I would go to heaven when I died, but I was desperate for some help to get through each day on earth with peace and joy. My soul was filled with pain from the abuse of my childhood and I manifested that pain daily in my attitudes and inability to maintain good relationships.

God's word tells us that if we seek Him diligently we will find Him (see Prov. 8:17). I began seeking God on my own for whatever I was missing, and I had an encounter with Him that brought me much closer to Him. He suddenly seemed very present in my daily life and I began to study diligently in order to know Him better. It seemed that everywhere I turned, I heard about faith. I learned that I could apply my faith in many circumstances, which would open a door for God to get involved and help me.

I believed with all my heart that the principles I was learning were correct, but I still experienced great frustration because I couldn't seem to get them to work for me, at least not to the degree to which I desperately needed them to work. At that time, God was using me in ministry, and my ministry to others was actually quite large. I had definitely made tremendous progress, but still felt deep within my heart that something was missing, so once again I began to seek God in a serious way. Through my searching and deeper study I learned that I was missing the main lesson Jesus came to teach us: to love God, love ourselves, and love others (see Matt. 22:36–39). I had learned a lot about faith as I walked with God, but I had not learned about the power of love.

Trust God and Do Good

During the several years of my journey of learning about this marvelous subject, I realized that faith only works through love. According to Galatians 5:6, faith is actually "activated and energized and expressed" through love.

The Holy Spirit led me to study Psalm 37:3: "Trust (lean on, rely on, and be confident) in the Lord and do good." I was startled to realize that I had only half of what I needed to know to connect properly with God. I had the faith (trust) part, but not the "do good" part. I wanted good things to happen to me, but I was not overly concerned about being good to others, particularly when I was hurting or going through a time of personal trial.

Psalm 37:3 opened my eyes to see that I had been trusting God, but I wasn't concentrating on doing good. Not only was I lacking in this area, but I realized that most of the other Christians I knew were probably in the same condition. We were all occupied "believing" God for the things we wanted. We prayed together and released our faith through the prayer of agreement, but we did not meet together and discuss what we could do for others while we were waiting for our needs to be met. We had faith, but it was not being energized by love!

I don't want to sound as though I was totally self-absorbed, because that wasn't the case. I was working in ministry and wanted to help people, but mixed in with my desire to help were a lot of impure motives. Being in ministry gave me a sense of self-worth and importance. It gave me position and a certain amount of influence, but God wanted me to do everything I did with a pure motive, and I still had a great deal to learn. There were times I did acts of kindness to help people, but helping others was not my number-one motivator. I needed to be much more aggressive and purposeful about loving others; it needed to be the main thing in my life, not a sideline.

Ask yourself what motivates you more than anything else, and answer honestly. Is it love? If it isn't, are you willing to change your focus to what is important to God?

I pray with all my heart that God causes these words to leap from this page into your heart. Learning the truth about the power of love was so life changing for me that I want everyone else to know it too. I am not suggesting that you don't know it, for the truth is you may know a great deal more about loving others than I do. But just in case you don't, I pray that what I share with you will ignite a fire in you and that it encourages you to be part of a Love Revolution that I believe has the power to change the world!

Keep Yourself and Others Stirred Up

Just imagine how different the world would be if each one of us who claims to know Christ would do one kind thing for someone else every day. The results would be astonishing. Now imagine what would happen if we all set a goal to do two loving, kind, beneficial things for someone else every day. I am sure you get the picture. The results would be amazing. The world would change rapidly because we really could overcome evil with good if we all made a commitment to live the way Jesus tells us to live.

You might be tempted to ask, "That will never happen, so why even try?" Don't let yourself be defeated through negative thinking before you even begin. I have already decided that I am going to do my part and pray for other people to do theirs. I will also talk to other people and encourage them to do as much as they possibly can for others. It would be awesome if a lot of our conversation were centered around ways we can help others and creative ideas about things to do for them.

I have three friends who flow in this amazing lifestyle and when we go to lunch or have coffee together, we often use our time to talk about things God has put on our hearts to do for others or creative ideas for fresh ways to be a blessing. I believe conversations like this are very pleasing to God and certainly

they are better than sitting around complaining about everything that's wrong in the world. I would like to challenge you
to take a lead role in the Love Revolution. Enlist the people you
know and invite them to a planning session on practical ways
to meet needs. Share the principles in this book with them and
find a target. Find someone who needs help and make a group
effort to help them.

The idea of encouraging others to be aggressive in doing good
works is not a new one. The writer of Hebrews talked about
it: "And let us consider and give attentive, continuous care to
watching over one another, studying how we may stir up (stimulate and incite) to love and helpful deeds and noble activities"
(Heb. 10:24).

Please notice that this verse says we should give *continuous*
care to watching over one another and actually study and think
about how we can stir others up to good works and do loving
and helpful deeds. He encouraged those he wrote to do the same
thing that I am encouraging you to do today. Can you imagine
how the devil would despise our actually getting together to
find creative ways to be good to one another? He would prefer that we judge, be critical, find fault, gossip, and complain.
I believe that doing the right thing will require forming new
habits and developing aggressive acts of love, but the results
will be wonderful.

Be Rich in Good Works

Paul instructed Timothy, a young preacher, to charge people "to
do good, to be rich in good works, to be liberal and generous of

heart, ready to share [with others]" (1 Tim. 6:18). It is obvious
by this that Paul felt people needed to be reminded to do these
things. The instruction to be aggressive in good works is one
worth reminding people of today. I encourage you not only to
remind others, but also to find ways to remind yourself. Keep a
good library of books and messages on the subject of love and
read or listen to them often. Do whatever you need to do in
order to make sure that you don't forget the thing that is the
most important to God.

I believe the world is watching Christians and that what they
see us do is very important. Peter encouraged believers to conduct themselves properly and honorably among Gentiles, the
unbelievers of the day. He said that even if the unbelievers were
inclined to slander the believers that they would eventually
come to glorify God if they saw their good works and loving
deeds (see 1 Pet. 2:12).

If your neighbors know you go to church every Sunday,
I can assure you that they also watch your behavior. When I
was growing up, our neighbors dutifully went to church. Actually, they went several times a week, but they also did lots of
things they should not have done. I recall my father often saying, "They are no better than I am; they get drunk, use bad language, tell dirty jokes, and have bad tempers, so they are just a
bunch of hypocrites." My dad was looking for an excuse anyway and their behavior just added fuel to the fire.

I certainly realize that as Christians we don't behave per-
fectly and that people who want an excuse to not believe in
Jesus or practice Christianity will always watch us and criticize
us, but we should do the best we can to not give them a reason
to judge us.

Look for Ways to Bless

I always try to be open for God to show me anything He might want me to do that could witness to others or be a blessing to someone. Just a few days ago, I was getting my nails done. A young girl was in the shop and she was very pregnant with her first child. She had been on bed rest for two months because of early labor pains and this trip to the nail salon was her first opportunity to get out of the house in quite some time. Her baby was actually due in a week and she was getting a manicure and pedicure. We chatted a little, and I started to feel that blessing her by paying for her services that day would be a nice gesture. I waited a bit just to see if the desire stayed with me and since it did, I paid for her services when I paid for my mine. She was, of course, surprised, but blessed. I didn't make a big deal out of it, I just did it. Maybe someday she will see me on television or see one of my books and remember that I actually did what I say I believe.

I don't do things like that to be seen, but what people do see speaks much louder to them than words alone. Everyone in the nail shop knows I am a Bible teacher and minister. Although I did not tell the young woman anything about myself, I am sure others told her after I left. So one little act of kindness accomplished several purposes. It made me happy; it made her happy; it was an example to others watching; and it was a witness that glorified God. I had another option. I could have kept my money and done nothing. That would have been easy, but not nearly as satisfying to my soul.

Don't Worry about What People Think

You might think, *Joyce, I would feel really odd just offering to pay a bill for someone I don't even know.* If you do, I understand completely. I do, too. I wonder what they think or how they'll respond, but then I remember that none of that is my concern. I am only concerned with being an ambassador for Christ.

One day, I tried to buy a cup of coffee for a woman who was in line behind me at Starbucks and she flatly refused. Actually, she made such a scene that it embarrassed me and at first I thought, *Well, I won't do that again.* Dave was with me, and he reminded me that was exactly what the devil wanted, so I changed my mind. Such times are not easy, but that incident made me sadly aware of how many people don't know how to receive a blessing—probably because it never happens to them.

Sometimes I do things anonymously, but at times I cannot hide what I do, so I have decided that as long as my heart is right, that is all that matters. Each act of kindness is my way of obeying God and overcoming the evil in the world. I don't know what kind of evil things have happened to people and perhaps my acts of kindness will help heal the wounds in their souls. I also believe kindness toward others is a way for me to get the devil back for the pain he caused in my life. He is evil to the maximum degree; he is the perpetrator of all the evil we experience in the world, so every act of love, goodness, and kindness is like stabbing him in his evil, wicked heart.

If you've been mistreated and often wished for a way you could get back at the devil for the pain he has caused you, then be good to as many people as you can. It is God's way, and it will work because love never fails!

I Purchased a Soul with Love

The Bible says that God purchased us with a precious price—the blood of His Son, Jesus Christ (see 1 Cor. 6:20, 1 Pet. 1:19, Rev. 5:9). This amazing act of goodness reversed the evil the devil had done and opened a way for all men to have their sins forgiven and enjoy a personal relationship with God.

As I have mentioned, my father abused me sexually for many years and his evil deeds damaged my soul and left me wounded and unable to function normally until Jesus healed me. Getting over what he did to me and being able to totally forgive him was a process. At first, I made the decision not to hate him anymore because God made me aware that love for Him and hate for my natural father could not dwell in the same heart. I asked God to help me and He did take the hatred from my heart. However, I still wanted very little to do with my father and stayed as far away from him as possible.

My mother's mental health was declining for years, and the year I married Dave she had a nervous breakdown as a result of knowing what my dad had done to me and not knowing how to deal with it. She had caught him abusing me when I was fourteen, but, as I said, she did not know what to do so she did nothing. Doing nothing turned out to be a very bad decision for all of us. For two years, she received shock treatments and they erased her memory of the sexual abuse and I did not want to do anything that would cause her to remember again, so even though it was hard for me to be around my father, my family visited on holidays and other times only when we absolutely had to.

Eventually, my parents moved out of town and returned to the small town where they grew up. It was about two hundred miles from where I lived and I was delighted because their move meant I would see them even less. I had managed to forgive my father at some point during those years, but I had not *totally* forgiven him.

As my parents got older and their health and money declined, God began dealing with me about moving them back to St. Louis, Missouri, where we live, and taking care of them until their deaths. That meant buying them a house, furniture, a car, and providing someone to clean their house, get their groceries, cut the lawn, and do household repairs. At first, I thought this idea was the devil trying to torment me, but eventually I realized it was God's plan and I can honestly say it was one of the single most difficult things I have ever done in my life.

First of all, Dave and I had a small amount of money saved and setting up my parents in a home would take almost all of it. Secondly, I did not think they deserved my help since they had never really done anything for me except abuse and abandon me. As Dave and I talked and prayed about it, I realized more and more that what God was asking me to do was not only the hardest thing He had ever asked of me, it would also be one of the most powerful things I had ever done.

I read every Scripture I could find on loving your enemies, being kind to them and doing them favors. This one really impacted me:

But love your enemies and be kind and do good [doing favors so that someone derives benefit from them] and lend, expecting and hoping for nothing in return but considering nothing as lost and despairing of no one; and then your recompense (your reward) will be great (rich, strong, intense, and abundant), and you will be sons of the

Most High, for He is kind and charitable and good to the
ungrateful and the selfish and wicked

(Luke 6:35).

This verse says we should consider nothing as lost and not
despair over any of it. Before I understood this principle, I had
looked at my childhood as lost years, now God was asking
me to see them as experience I could use to help others. Luke
also said we should ask blessings on and pray for those who
abuse and misuse us (see Luke 6:28). This seems so unfair, but
I have since learned that when I forgive I am doing myself a
favor. When I forgive, I set myself free from all the results of the
wrong done to me and then God can deal with the entire situation. If my enemy is unsaved, I may just purchase a soul.

My father was quite overwhelmed by the offer Dave and I
extended and although he never said so, I know he wondered
why in the world we would do so much for him after what he
had done to me.

Three years went by and I saw no change in him. He was
still mean, easily angered, and very selfish. Actually, there were
times when he seemed to be getting worse as far as his temper-
ment was concerned. I realize now that God was dealing with
him all that time. Three years after we did what God asked us
to do, my dad repented with tears and accepted Jesus as His
Savior. It was quite a wonderful experience. He initiated the
whole thing. He asked us to come to his house, and he asked
for forgiveness. He asked Dave and me both to forgive him and
made mention of how good we had been to him. We asked if he
wanted to invite Jesus into his life and not only did he do that,
but he also asked if Dave and I would baptize him. I had the

privilege of seeing my father, who abused me, come to know the Lord. Then I realized that I had previously thought I was purchasing a house, some furniture, and a car, but actually I had purchased a soul with an act of undeserved kindness.

During this time, Dave and I also saw our ministry grow in an amazing way, enabling us to help a lot more people. I believe this growth was part of the harvest on the seed of obedience we had sown. When God asks us to do difficult things, He always does so for our benefit and for the benefit of His Kingdom. You see, we really can overcome evil with good. So as John Wesley said: "Do all the good you can, by all the means you can, in all the ways you can, in all the places you can, at all the times you can, to all the people you can, as long as ever you can."

Widows of War

Jennifer hears the cries of the children and she comes running to their rescue. As she's done so many times before, she tells them that everything is going to be all right. As their mother, she'll keep telling them until they believe it.

She knows what it's like to be afraid, abducted, and abused. When she was just twelve, she was taken by force from her home, ripped from her family and her village by rebel soldiers involved in Africa's longest war. After continual beatings, rape, and intense labor, Jennifer's will to live gave her the courage to escape. And with her, she led others to safety.

But when she returned home, her family was gone. Alone and desperate for a new life and a home she could call her own, she married a man who already had a wife. On her wedding day, he physically beat and cut her in front of her friends. But the cruelest blow was yet to come. On a special day that should have made her feel like a princess, treasured and loved, he told everyone assembled that she was useless and a disgrace. The words drove deep, creating pain far greater than the physical beatings that continued.

Eventually, her husband died of AIDS, and again, she was alone. As a widow with two children of her own, she asked God, *"Are You there? Will my life be nothing but torment, suffering, and shame?"* God proved His faithfulness to Jennifer and she is in the process of total restoration.

Today, Jennifer lives in safety at a new village provided by Watoto Ministries, in partnership with Joyce Meyer Ministries. With restored dignity and purpose for her life, she is now caring for children orphaned by the war. Unfortunately, many others are still in desperate need of healing and restoration.

God's word repeatedly tells us to care for the widow and the orphan. It seems that God has a special place in His heart for them and we should also.

Statistics say:

- In many countries, widows whose husbands died of AIDS are evicted from their homes and subjected to extreme forms of violence.[1]
- Households headed by widows often represent one of the poorest subgroups in Africa.[2]

CHAPTER

7

Justice for the Oppressed

Justice consists not in being neutral between right and
wrong, but in finding out the right and upholding it,
wherever found, against the wrong.

Theodore Roosevelt

God is a God of justice. In fact, justice is one of my favorite
qualities of His. Simply put, it means He makes wrong things
right. The Bible says that righteousness and justice are the
foundation of His throne (see Ps. 89:14). A foundation is what
a building stands on, so we might say that all of God's activity
in the earth rests on the fact that He is righteous and just. As
God's servants, we are instructed to love righteousness and justice and work to establish it on earth.

The absence of justice in a society always leads to trouble. From
1789 to 1799 France experienced a revolution. It was a bloody war
in which the peasants rose up against the aristocrats and religious
leaders of the day. As long as the king and queen of France were

treating the people rightly and justly, their kingdom flourished; however when the king and queen selfishly allowed widespread malnutrition, starvation, and disease while they taxed the people and continued to live lavish lifestyles, the people eventually revolted against them. When they treated the citizens unjustly, the foundation of their throne cracked and was eventually destroyed.

The truth is simply that without justice, things don't work properly. Our society today is filled with injustice and although some people work hard to fight against it, the majority of people either don't care or, if they do care, they simply don't know what to do about it.

It's Our Duty

Who cares for orphans, widows, the poor, and the oppressed? God does, but do we? When people are oppressed, they have a

> Who cares for orphans, widows, the poor, and the oppressed?

burden that is unreasonable; it overwhelms, overpowers, and depresses them. Their burdens often cause them to be without hope. God is a Father to the fatherless and a defender of widows (see Ps. 68:5). He seems to have a special place in His heart for people who are lonely and have no one to take care of them. God helps the afflicted, and secures justice for the poor and needy (see Ps. 140:12). I am sure you are glad that God helps these hurting people, but I urge you to remember that God does

His work through people who are submitted to Him. Now ask yourself what you are personally doing for them.

As I mentioned earlier, more than two thousand Scriptures in the Bible speak of our duty to the poor and needy. Since God inspired that many, there must be a message He is trying to make sure we understand. How important is it for each of us to be involved in some way in helping afflicted people? Probably more important than many of us realize.

True Religion

The apostle James said that true religion that is expressed in outward acts is to "visit and help and care for the orphans and widows in their affliction" (James 1:27). That means if our religion is real, then we will get involved in helping those who are oppressed by the circumstances of their lives. I can only conclude from this verse that if I am not helping these people, then my religion must not be true. It may be a form of religion, but certainly it is not fully what God intends it to be.

I have learned that not everyone who sits in a church on Sunday is a real Christian as far as God is concerned. Following rules, regulations, and doctrines does not make one a true believer in Jesus Christ. How can I say that? Because when we receive Christ as our Savior we receive the heart of God and we receive His Spirit (see Ezek. 11:19); that being the case, we have to learn to care about what God cares about—and He cares about helping hurting people.

What good would it do for my sons, who manage most of the daily business of Joyce Meyer Ministries, to say they have my heart if they were not going to do what I would do in a situation? The very reason we have our sons in the positions they are in is that they know us intimately and have the same heart we do concerning helping people.

Love One Another

I believe very strongly that we need to love one another, meaning those we are in contact with in our personal lives, and also those we may never meet personally, who live in far away places (see Acts 2:44–45, Acts 4:31–32, 2 Cor. 8:1–4). I would like you to keep both of these groups of people in mind as we continue this book. For example, you could give financially to support an orphan in a third-world country through a ministry who cares for them and you could also invite a widow in your church to lunch and while you are with her ask enough questions to make sure her needs are being met adequately. If she mentions that she has a need that you can meet then do it cheerfully, for God loves a cheerful giver (2 Cor. 9:7).

Most of us would help our families or people we know intimately if they were in need, but the farther removed people are from our personal circles, the less likely we are to care about them or be willing to get involved in helping them. I believe God wants to change that. I realize that as an individual I cannot fully meet every need I hear about, but I can certainly be open to letting God show me if there is something I can do. I am determined to no longer just assume I can't do anything about the needs I become aware of. I have come to realize that is a passive way of looking at needs, and not the way God wants me to approach them.

The World Needs the Church to Be the Church

Jesus asked Peter three times if he loved Him and all three times, when Peter said, "Yes," Jesus answered with, "Then feed My sheep" or "Feed My lambs" (see John 21:15–17). Jesus was not speaking of feeding animals; He was talking about helping His people. On several occasions He referred to Himself as a shepherd and to His people as sheep, so Peter knew exactly what He was talking about.

It seems to me that Jesus is saying in these verses that if we love Him we should be helping other people, not simply gathering in buildings on Sunday morning to follow rules and rituals. Of course, we should want to go to church to fellowship, worship God and learn, but church should also be a place *from* which we help others. If a church is not involved in reaching the lost around the world and helping oppressed people including widows, orphans, the poor and needy, then I am not at all sure they have the right to call themselves a church.

People by the tens of thousands have stopped going to church, and spiritual leaders worldwide are concerned about the decline in church attendance. I believe the reason for this decline is largely that many churches have become religious centers with no real life in them. The apostle John said that we know we have passed over out of death into life by the fact that we love the brethren and he who does not love is held and kept continually in spiritual death (see 1 John 3:14). If a church is not overflowing with the genuine love of God, how can it be filled with life?

I have heard that in Europe another cathedral or church building closes almost every week and that many of them are being purchased by Muslim groups and turned into mosques. Surely that is not God's intended destiny for the church of Jesus Christ. A lot of great churches are doing exactly what they should be doing and they are growing and full of life because of it. But, it is safe to say, they are the exception and not the majority of churches.

The early church, which we read about in the book of Acts, was a very powerful church. It shook the known world of its time and its influence is still being felt around the world today. It was unified and all the people who were part of it were busy helping the people they knew to be in need. They helped those they knew personally and those they heard about in other towns and cities through the apostles who came to visit and teach them.

The early church grew rapidly and had a wonderful reputation because it was filled with people who genuinely loved one another. What the world needs is love, not religion! It needs God; and God is love. If we agree and all get involved we can start a Love Revolution, a movement that will shake the world once again for the glory of God!

Learn to Do Right

It is simply wrong to see or hear of someone in need and do absolutely nothing. Isaiah the prophet said: "Learn to do right! Seek justice, relieve the oppressed, and correct the oppressor, Defend the fatherless, plead for the widow" (Isa. 1:17).

The purpose of teaching and instruction is to help us learn what is right and encourage us to do it. Just a few years ago, I had no idea how strongly God felt about my working to bring justice to the oppressed, but once I did learn, I started doing it.

God has been instructing people how to treat the fatherless, the widows, the oppressed and the poor since He gave the law, in Old Testament times. Speaking through Moses, He said, "You shall not afflict any widow or fatherless child" (Exod. 22:22). God is not partial, "He executes justice for the fatherless and the widow, and loves the stranger or temporary resident and gives him food and clothing" (Deut. 10:18). God told the people that if they fed the stranger, the temporary resident, the widow and the fatherless, He would bless the work of their hands (see Deut. 14:29). Please notice that all of these groups—widows, strangers, the fatherless—would probably be full of very lonely people. God cares about the lonely!

Lonely and Forgotten

I cannot imagine how lonely and forgotten an orphan girl who has been forced into prostitution in order to survive feels.

Statistics say:

- Two million girls between ages five and fifteen are introduced into the commercial sex market each year.
- 89 percent of prostitutes want to escape.
- At least two hundred thousand women and children work in prostitution in Thailand and one third of them are under the age of eighteen. Girls as young as six years old work as prostitutes.
- One time, a doctor found thirty-five men using a girl in one hour.

Are all of these girls orphans? No, not all of them are official orphans in terms of not having any parents. But, they are orphans in God's eyes because they either have no parents or the parents they have can't or don't want to take care of them.

Teen Prostitution

Sell your body for the pleasure of evil men or die of starvation. It's a terrible choice that no one should ever have to make. Though she's just nineteen years old, Birtukan has made this choice since she was fourteen. And with every choice, her heart breaks a little more and her soul is destroyed. With all she's been through, it's a miracle she still feels anything at all.

She finds strength when she gazes into the eyes of her seven-month-old daughter, Aamina. *"I make this choice because I don't want my daughter to do the same."* Her Ethiopian name, Aamina, means *"safe,"* and Birtukan has decided she'll do whatever it takes to keep her promise to keep her daughter safe.

She does not sell her body for greed or self-pleasure. She sells her body to survive. She lives and performs her work in a four-by-nine-foot room. She's worked for five years— no days off…no vacation…no rest. She closes her eyes and thinks about Aamina, while as many as fifteen men a day abuse her body to satisfy their evil desires. The pain is unimaginable, but it is the only way she knows to provide food and a place to sleep. When she thinks of how much she loves Aamina, she can't comprehend how her own mother could have abandoned her when she was just five years old.

Before she came to what is referred to as the red-light district in Addis Ababa, she was dying of starvation. *"I had hope, but that hope seems far from me now. I know God is with me and loves me. I don't know any other way to live."* A faint glimmer of hope remains for a day when survival won't cost her a piece of her heart, her soul, and her damaged body.

Today, those hopes will have to wait. Her next customer just arrived.

Statistics[1] say:

- The average age of entry into prostitution worldwide is thirteen to fourteen years old.
- 75 percent of prostitutes are under the age of twenty-five.

Seeing a New Level of Degradation and Doing Something about It

When I went to India, to the red-light district (the prostitution area) in one of the slums, I was introduced to a new level of degradation. Not only was the entire area filthy beyond description, it was also filled with brothels. I was taken into one that consisted of three small rooms with three beds in each room. None of these bed areas had any privacy at all. The girls or women serviced men in these small rooms mainly at night, hoping to make enough money to be able to eat and feed their children if they had any, and many of them did. Where were their children while they worked? They either played in the hallway where they could easily access the rooms their moms were in or they were given alcohol to put them to sleep so they could not bother their mothers. A few of them had learned about our feeding and school program and we were able to care for them during these hours so they did not have to witness what was going on at home. Home! These little children live in brothels!

Without help, most of the female children—*little girls*—will merely transition into the life of prostitution as soon as they are old enough. These women don't live like this because they want to; they have no other choice. They are uneducated and have grown up in the midst of poverty that most of us would not even begin to understand. Some of them are actually owned by pimps who, for all intents and purposes, keep them prisoners and beat them if they don't make enough money.

I am happy to say that we have initiated a program to help rescue them. First, we have been working in this area for at least three years alongside some other local ministries, and the number of prostitutes has dropped from three thousand to three hundred. Some people just need a little hope or help, and they need someone to tell them they can make a change and show them how to do it.

Our ministry has purchased several hundred acres of property about three hours away from the red-light district, and we have built a village complete with a training center to teach these women a trade that will enable them to support themselves and their families without resorting to prostitution. We moved the first one hundred women and children to the Restoration Center in February 2008 and intend to move all of those who want to make a change.

It was so heartwarming for me to listen to the little girls and especially the teenagers giggle out loud when I showed them the shower and toilet facilities they would have. You see, they had never taken a bath in any way other than pouring a bucket of water over themselves behind a building somewhere. To be able to be part of putting smiles on their faces and giving them hope is an amazing feeling. It definitely feels better than the selfish, self-centered way I once lived. The partners of our ministry are largely responsible for this outreach in India because it is their faithful giving that pays for it, and we appreciate them deeply.

I might add that some of the older women trapped in prostitution are widows. Their husbands have died or have been killed in some instances and left them with no means of support, so once again they resort to the only thing they can think of to make money.

We can learn to do what is right to help the oppressed in the world. All we need is information and determination and we can make a positive difference in many people's lives. If each of us will do our part we can start a revolution of love.

Injustice Is Everywhere

Injustice abounds not only in third-world countries but also in our neighborhoods and cities everywhere. There are people we work with who have desperate needs. We walk by them on the street and we encounter them at the marketplace. Injustice has many faces. It may be seen in the face of a woman whose husband left her with three small children for another woman. It may be in the face of a girl or boy who was sexually or physically abused while growing up by parents or other adults. It may be seen in the face of a father raised in the ghetto, who is a third-generation family member living on welfare. He would like to live better, but he honestly doesn't even begin to know what to do. He has very little education and has never even seen anyone live any differently than he does except perhaps on television.

Some people do overcome and rise up out of the tragedy of injustice, but many don't. Perhaps they need you or me or someone we know to invest in them. Our inner city ministry works in the public schools to help children learn to read and write. We have asked for volunteers to help tutor the children and it is discouraging to think about how few people are willing to even give an hour a week for something like this. Of course, we think, "Someone" should certainly help these children, but somehow we are not the ones to show up and do the helping! We have our excuses and they soothe our consciences, but are they acceptable to God? For years, I made excuses about everything I did not want to do, but I have discovered a truth that has become one of my favorite sayings: "Indifference makes excuses; love finds a way."

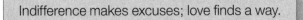

Indifference makes excuses; love finds a way.

The Standard for Righteousness

In the Bible, beginning in the Old Testament, we see one example after another of people who were very involved in helping the poor and needy. Job was one of those people. He said that by being eyes to the blind, feet to the lame, and a father to the poor and needy, he had put on righteousness (see Job 29:14–16). The phrase "put on" has a specific meaning that we don't want to miss. Think of it this way: When I put on my clothes, I do so on purpose. I don't stand passively in my closet and wait for them to jump off the hangers and onto my body. I carefully select each piece and not only do I put it on, but I also make sure it looks good on me.

God said that Job was a righteous man and Job said that he "put on" righteousness. In other words, he did it on purpose. The standard for righteousness in Job's day demanded helping widows, orphans, the poor and needy, and all who were oppressed.

In our society today we don't have many standards left. It seems that a majority of people just do what they feel like doing, and selfishness rules. We need standards that produce men and women of integrity, truth, honesty, honor, faithfulness, loyalty, and genuine care for hurting people. If more people had such qualities, our world would be a completely different place. Your response might be, "Yes, I wish we did have that today," but don't forget that wishing does no good at all. We must take action. Our world will be changed only as the people in it change—and that change has to start with each one of us. We must all carry the torch and say, "I am the Love Revolution!"

Esther, the young Jewish maiden you read about in chapter four, who eventually became a queen, commanded that gifts be sent to the poor when she and her countrymen celebrated their freedom. Part of our celebrating the good things that God has done for us should be to remember to reach out to those who are still in need. A friend of mine is on a committee in her church that reaches out to homeless shelters at Christmas. The church gets a list of all the children living at a particular shelter, complete with the children's ages and clothing sizes. Church members who are able to do so choose a child's name and purchase a

Christmas gift just for that child. In December, a Christmas party is held at the shelter where there's lots of food, Christmas music, stories about Jesus' birth and His love for each child, and, of course, the gifts are given to each child.

After the party the church members feel good about helping the homeless children, but many have also said that when they return home after the party, they're more grateful for their own homes and blessings than they were before the party.

It is very good for us to see and experience the needs of others firsthand because it brings a fresh awareness of how blessed we are. Hopefully it also makes us realize how much we could be doing if we put forth an effort. People tend to get more generous at Christmas time and many people do try to help someone else, but we need to realize that the poor and marginalized are needy all the time, and not just once a year at Christmas.

As I write today Dave and I are in a hotel that has an extremely small bathroom and shower. It is so small that Dave's head touches the ceiling. At first he murmured just a tiny bit about the discomfort, but then he remembered the people we have met who have no water and have to walk hours just to bring home enough dirty water to help their families survive. These people rarely take baths and if they do it is not in a bathroom with a shower. We have both discovered that reaching out to needy people is a blessing to us because it helps us not to murmur and complain, but to give thanks in all things as God wants us to do.

Boaz, a wealthy man and leader in his community left what the Bible calls handfuls on purpose (Ruth 2:16) in his fields for Ruth to find and collect to be used to feed herself and her mother-in-law. Both Ruth and Naomi were widows and they were poor. The law in that day commanded that not all the grain be harvested from the fields. The people had to leave some for the poor to come and glean out of the fields so they too could eat. We see over and over that God always provided for the poor. But His provision did not fall out of the sky or just miraculously appear; He provided through people.

Love in Action

At Joyce Meyer Ministries, we have an account called "Love in Action." The ministry and employees can give money to this account specifically to be used for the needs of fellow employees who might be experiencing a difficult time financially for one reason or another. Perhaps sickness has left them with a burden, or a special need with a child may have gotten them in distress. We decided we wanted to be prepared to help those among us who had genuine needs and could not help themselves.

If you have a Bible study group or even a group of friends interested in being part of the Love Revolution, one thing you can do is select a treasurer or open a special bank account and let everyone donate to that special fund each week or month. You can call it "Love in Action," if you want to or choose your own name, but use it to meet needs that arise. Often we hear about needs and wish we had more money. Why not start saving for those times so you can be prepared? If you cannot find a group that is interested, then find one or two people and if you have to, do it by yourself, but refuse to do nothing!

Why Do I Need My Arm if I Don't Use It to Help Somebody?

One of the shocking statements I discovered while studying how Job responded to the poor was his observation that if he did not use his arm to help the hurting, then somebody should pull it off his body (see Job 31:21–22). This caused me to realize just how serious he was about helping people. Am I willing to be that serious? Are you?

Is there any real purpose in being alive if all we are going to do is get up every day and live only for ourselves? I have tried that and found that it left me empty and unfulfilled. I don't think that is what God has in mind for us at all as His representatives here on earth.

I stopped writing this manuscript for a little while to re-read all the Scriptures I could find on loving others. Now I am even more convinced than ever that this is the real purpose in living. I urge you to dedicate your entire being to doing good. Offer God your hands, arms, mouth, feet, eyes, and ears and ask Him to use them to make someone else's life better. Use your arms to reach out with a hand of hope to someone who is hungry, in pain, or lonely.

The Harvest of Love

Giving and living selflessly do produce a harvest in our lives. There is nothing wrong with desiring and expecting a harvest. Our motivation for helping others should not be to get something for ourselves, but God does tell us we will reap what we sow and we can look forward to that benefit. One Scripture that expresses this truth so beautifully is found in the book of Luke 6:38: "Give, and it shall be given unto you; good measure, pressed down, and shaken together, and running over, shall men give into your bosom. For with the same measure that ye mete withal it shall be measured to you again" (KJV).

God promises to reward those who diligently seek Him (see Heb. 11:6). The word *reward* in the original Greek text of the New Testament means, "wages received in this life" or "recompense." In the Hebrew language, in which the Old Testament is written, the word *reward* means, "fruit, earnings, product, price, or result." The word *reward* is used 68 times in the Amplified version of the Bible. God wants us to look forward to rewards of our obedience and good choices.

If we care about those who are poor and oppressed, God promises that we will not want, but that if we hide our eyes from their need we shall have "many a curse" in our lives (Prov. 28:27). The writer of Proverbs even says that when we give to the poor we are lending to God (see Prov. 19:17). I cannot imagine that God does not pay great interest on what is loaned to Him.

I urge you to work to bring justice to the oppressed. That simply means that when you see something that you know is not right, you work to make it right.

Living in the Light

We all probably want more light in our lives. That would mean more clarity, better understanding, and less confusion. The prophet Isaiah declared that if we would divide our bread with the hungry and bring the homeless poor into our homes, cover the naked and stop hiding ourselves from the needs around us, our light would break forth (see Isa. 58:7–8). He also said that our healing and restoration and the power of a new life would spring quickly. That sounds good to me and I am sure it does to do you also.

Isaiah wrote of justice and said it would go before us and conduct us to peace and prosperity and that the glory of the Lord would be our rear guard. If we are actively helping the oppressed, God goes before us and He also has our back! I like that feeling of safety and certainty.

Isaiah further said that if we would pour out that with which we sustain our own lives for the hungry and satisfy the need of the afflicted that our light would rise in darkness and any gloom we experienced would be comparable to the sun at noon (see Isa. 58:10). The sun is very bright at noon, so it sounds to me like helping people is the way to live in the light.

The Lord will guide us continually and even in dry times He will satisfy us. He will make our bones strong and our lives will be like a watered garden (see Isa. 58:11). All of this happens as a result of living to bring justice to the oppressed.

I hope you are seeing what I am seeing through these promises. I think most of us waste a lot of our lives trying to get what God will gladly give if we simply do what He is asking us to do. Care about the poor, the hungry, the destitute, orphans, widows, the oppressed and needy. Live your life to help others, and God will satisfy you in every way possible.

LOVE REVOLUTIONARY
Martin Smith

What Does Our Love Revolve Around?

I remember it all so clearly. It was January 10, 2008. The side street—all potholes and no sidewalks—was just big enough for our bus to squeeze through. We stepped out into heat and chaos and the smell of a thousand used tires dumped on a fire already blended with cheap fuel and last month's trash. Stalls and workshops and shacks and homes. Saris and sandals and bare feet and a noise that blurred the senses.

But all this was as nothing compared to what came next...

This was Mumbai, India. We were in a slum, or, to be precise, we were in a red-light district of one of the city's many slums. There were no red lights to see, and everybody there seemed to be occupied in some way—making, selling, sweeping, carrying.

We were here to see Prem Kiran—a project devoted to working with children of prostitutes and their families. Dave and Joyce had invited us. They told us it was a project we really ought to see for ourselves.

I don't know that I'd ever encountered quite so much life in one single room. It was as if the walls were unable to hold it all. Seventy smiling faces, all turned toward the visitors like sunflowers toward the evening sun. Outside, I could see the street and the slum and the alleys down which so much pain and struggle and death lurked. But being inside this room was an experience more potent than any I had ever tasted.

There was one child in particular whom I felt unable to leave. Farin (pronounced *fa-reen*) was her name and there was something about her that told me I'd have trouble walking away from her.

I found out more over the next hour. Like most of the others, Farin's mother was a prostitute. Prem Kiran had stepped in and helped to make her life so much better—offering food, clothing, education, and the support of loving, devoted, sacrificial Christians. Yet my mind was plagued by questions.

How many times had Farin had to hide beneath the bed while her mother worked?

How much danger had she been exposed to in the slum's streets after dark?

How could her life hope to be much different if she didn't get out now?

How could I walk away?

How could I?

That one afternoon in Mumbai changed everything.

The next evening we were playing a concert in the city. What else could we do but get the children and their mothers to come join us on stage? So they came, and it was great to have them up there with us—all shy smiles and adrenaline jumps and culture shock. And then something bigger happened. We played, and the mothers simply started to dance. The mothers of the night, the sex workers who were dressed in red lipstick and faded saris, danced with freedom and grace and love in front of a crowd of thousands. Spinning like falling feathers, hands that told stories and feet that trod with care; their dance captured something I'd never seen before.

And that's when it struck me: Where should justice be?

Where should the outcasts be welcome? Where should those whose lives are weighed down by poverty find freedom and hope? Where should our love get spent without question?

I'd been brought up in church, but somewhere along the way I'd missed some lessons. I'd not learned that when it comes to our response to poverty and injustice—and the role of us Christians as worshippers—God doesn't want things neatly divided. Years back I would have run a mile from the suggestion that we should have a group of women who were forced into prostitution dancing on stage while we worshipped. Now it seems like a sign of the times. It seems that God is stirring the church up like never before and letting us know that it is just these types of people who need to be welcome.

So when it comes to dealing with the idea of how we are in need of a Love Revolution, I'm left with one question: What does our love revolve around?

I got home from the trip to Mumbai and everything was a mess. My head had stopped working the way it used to, and I was deeply troubled. I felt a burden on me when it came to Farin—that if we didn't do something ourselves her life would head toward a future made short by suffering, poverty, abuse, and disease. I felt as though she had become another daughter and our family was incomplete without her.

It turns out that God's plans were different from mine.

A year and a few months later, as I write about this experience, things are not quite the way I had assumed they would be. Farin has not left the city. She's still with her family, but her mother no longer works as a prostitute. They're about to move a few hours out of Mumbai, to live in a community for people just like them—ex-sex workers wanting to find new life away from the chaos and danger of the past. Farin's life is looking fuller than I could have hoped.

And mine?

In a way, I was kind of right about becoming a father again. But not to Farin. Sometime this year my wife, Anna, and I gave birth to another child—a charity, called CompassionArt.

CompassionArt exists to raise money through arts-related projects (like albums and books) that use sales and royalties to fight poverty in all its forms, the extreme sort that robs people of life and the sort that might be harder to spot but robs people of hope. We both remember talking to Joyce and Dave about it at its conception, which I guess makes them CompassionArt's grandparents or something like that. It was their passion and wisdom that helped us take those early steps.

But more than that, CompassionArt is about reworking the formula. It's about challenging the math that suggests that when we cease to care for others our faith remains on course. It doesn't. The truth, of course, is that it all just gets weaker. When our passion and purpose and love revolve around our own agenda, we have simply got it wrong.

When our love reaches out beyond us we find ourselves aligned more closely with God's right way up.

Lately whenever I've found myself with a microphone, a stage, and a crowd, wondering what's coming next, I've felt a need to read from Isaiah 58. Somehow I've been unable to resist the simplicity and strength of the words, and even though they were hand delivered to the Israelites a little less than three thousand years ago, they deal with eternal issues that are just as relevant today.

I get caught up in the passion of the opening lines: "Shout

it aloud, do not hold back. Raise your voice like a trumpet"
(Isa. 58:1 NIV).

What follows deserves to be screamed, not whispered or
filed away for a later date. This is a real-time issue that must
capture the attention of everyone, everywhere: "Day after day
they seek me out; they seem eager to know my ways, *as if* they
were a nation that does what is right and has not forsaken the
commands of its God. They ask me for just decisions and *seem*
eager for God to come near them" (v. 2 NIV, emphasis mine). It's
those words *seem* and *as if* that are the problem. Their heart's
clearly not right and they're heading for a fall.

God answers their question about why He seems to have
ignored all their premium quality religious acts: "On the day of
your fasting, you do as you please and exploit all your workers . . . You cannot fast as you do today and expect your voice
to be heard on high" (vv. 3–4 NIV).

Then come the lessons once again, the recapping so that even
those of us who have been dozing at the back finally get it: "Is not
this the kind of fasting I have chosen: to loose the chains of injustice . . . to set the oppressed free . . . to share your food with the hungry and to provide the poor wanderer with shelter—when you see
the naked, to clothe him, and not to turn away from your own flesh
and blood?" (vv. 6–8 NIV). It really doesn't get much clearer, does
it? The persecuted, the abused, the hungry, the homeless, the
poor—these are the people around whom our love must revolve,
not ourselves or our failed ideas of being impressively religious.

God is clear about the result of all this: "Then your light will
break forth like the dawn, and your healing will quickly appear . . .
Then you will call, and the Lord will answer; you will cry for help,
and he will say: Here am I" (vv. 8–9 NIV).

For years we've searched for intimacy in our worship. We've sung songs that talk about God being close and our lives being His. We've pursued those moments when we know that God is close; we've chased after His voice and searched for His plans. And all along we've missed the key to true intimacy: "If you do away with the yoke of oppression, with the pointing finger and malicious talk, and if you spend yourselves in behalf of the hungry and satisfy the needs of the oppressed . . . The LORD will guide you always; he will satisfy your needs in a sun-scorched land and will strengthen your frame. You will be like a well-watered garden, like a spring whose waters never fail" (vv. 9–11 NIV).

And if we do, then more than the payoff of hearing God's voice and carrying His love to those that need it most, more than that fantastic image of being like a well-watered garden soaked in life itself, Isaiah makes clear that God's people start to take up their place in history: "Your people will rebuild the ancient ruins and will raise up the age-old foundations; you will be called Repairer of Broken Walls, Restorer of Streets with Dwellings" (v. 12 NIV).

And there's even more: "Then you will find your joy in the LORD, and I will cause you to ride on the heights of the land and to feast on the inheritance of your father Jacob" (v. 14 NIV).

And all of this from stopping trying to impress God with our attempts at being "spiritual" and having good services that impress those around us. All of this from feeding someone who is hungry, from giving clothes to the poor, from defending the powerless, and speaking up for the weak. All of this—all of this history—gets made—from the simplest of acts. If only—if only we can learn to love more than ourselves.

There's another truth behind all of this. The fact is, it can be hard to look out and try to make our love revolve around others. It's easier when it's all about us. Why? Partly because it's always been this way—from stories of couples tasting forbidden fruit to kings on rooftops spying soon-to-be widows, and bad-tempered prophets heading to Spain because they couldn't face the prospect of God's extending mercy to anyone but His own people. This is the way it has always been with us, the continual struggle as we place ourselves on the throne instead of God and His *Outrospective* approach to life.

It seems as if it's perhaps a little harder than ever these days. All around are forces pushing us to obey our thirst, to give in to our impulses because "we're worth it," to take hold of life and make it in our own image. We're meant to want—and try to have—it all: the looks, the clothes, the income, the home, the relationships, the career. Everything designed to polish us up and make our lives so much better.

But we know the truth about life, don't we? We know that in spite of the pressure to conform, a life revolved around us cannot lead us to true happiness.

I always liked it when we played a gig and we got to sing our song about being a historymaker. Over the years in the band, we've sung it hundreds of times, feeling that the lines had a sort of power to leave people feeling inspired, pumped, and primed to get on and live a remarkable life that would make history. But there is more; there has to be more.

If we're going to be historymakers—and the future of millions of lives depends on there being more and more of us out there that are signing up to do so—then for most of us, it will be for a pretty specific set of reasons. We will make history by choosing to live our lives as a series of small acts of selfless living. As Mother Teresa said, "There are no great things; only small things with great love." If we can get that into our DNA, the two billion Christians in the world could end world poverty in a matter of weeks. That's the kind of history I want to see us making. Forget the inward focus; and just like those ancient words of Isaiah 58 promise, we will hear God more clearly and be in closer step with His power and His purpose if we stop making all this about ourselves and start to simply fix the problems and meet the needs that are around us. It's as simple as that.

What I know for sure is this; big will always be powerful but small is extremely beautiful. This Love Revolution has the power to be massive, but it will only ever be made up of those small acts of selfless, sacrificial love. So our big stages and big album sales and big songs—well, they're okay at best, but they're nothing as exciting as the power of a life lived against the flow.

One last point. How does the music fit into all this? The temptation to leave everything creative behind and go live in a cardboard box is strong. It feels as if this would be a way of finally doing something "real" with our lives. But this is never the whole story. A human's well-being relates to the whole—body, soul, and spirit. I've seen firsthand the power of music, and I'm convinced that it is God's secret weapon. Music can unite where there is war, it can soothe the pain of brokenness, it can break the hardest—and soothe the most broken—of hearts, from Rwandan genocide victims to New Yorkers who lost family in the twin towers, as well as those whose hatred ignited so much suffering.

Bring God into the equation—not that you can ever actually leave Him out, but you know what I mean, yes?—and you get a crowd beneath the Indian sky singing "God" songs, worshipping the Almighty with the angels. Open your eyes and you see healing come. Maybe it doesn't immediately put food into the mouths of desperate children, but it's a moment when heaven touches earth, and in that moment restoration happens. It is then that we feel a belonging, we feel that we are not alone. Incredibly, we feel that God Himself has not abandoned us.

Music can do this and God is not calling us to lay it aside and go live in a cardboard box. He is calling us to use our music, which is the gift He has placed in us to help the poor who live in desperate situations. If we adopt those lessons so clearly taught by the words in Isaiah, I'm convinced that in the coming days we will see great miracles before a note is even sung.

It's a music and Love Revolution.

Steven Curtis Chapman, a songwriter and worship leader and a man who inspires with every breath he takes and leads with humility and grace, once put things into great perspective for me. He may have sold millions of albums and been on the receiving end of countless award-show handshakes, but ask him what he's most proud of or humbled by and he'll tell you it's this—the way his family have given themselves over to adopting children in need of a home. "It's the clearest sign that God is at work in my life," he says.

When we look out beyond ourselves, when our love for others pushes us beyond the comfortable, when we place our treasure in rebuilding lives, it is then that we find ourselves living among the clearest signs that God is at work in our lives.

So this is one revolution that will not be televised. If we get it right, it won't need to be; the evidence of love in action will be blazed all over our lives, transforming our neighborhoods and breathing hope into the atmosphere.

It's as simple as that.

CHAPTER
8

Love Is Inclusive, Not Exclusive

If you judge people, you have no time to love them.
Mother Teresa

Jamie walked into the church on the corner of Spruce Avenue and Twenty-third Street in Harbor, Illinois. She was desperate for help. She had seen the church building for a long time and watched the people file in and out two or three times a week. Jamie had often sat in the coffee shop across the street from the church, drinking a latte, wondering how she would be accepted if she ever got up the nerve to go to one of the church services.

Jamie had been to Sunday school a few times as a child when she attended with a neighbor, but she certainly knew very little about the proper protocol of church attendance. She wasn't sure she would fit in or be accepted, so she just drank her coffee and watched. She tried to see if the church people looked any happier when they came out than they did when they went in, but they all left so quickly she couldn't really see clearly. Occasionally, someone from the church service came to the coffee shop after church. A few of them sat alone and, honestly, they looked as lonely as she felt. Some came with other people and they laughed and seemed happy, which gave her hope that she might one day have enough courage to go to a service.

Jamie grew up in a home where she received very little affection. Both of her parents were alcoholics and although they did not overtly abuse her, they did great damage to her self-image by being quick to criticize and find fault with her. They often compared her to her brother, who seemed to be smarter and more talented than she was in every way. She always felt unloved, ugly, and stupid, and as though she had no value at all.

By the time she was thirteen, Jamie had fallen in with the wrong crowd and was drinking and taking drugs. Her emotional pain was so deep that she numbed it with substance abuse. She also developed an eating disorder called bulimia. She ate normal amounts of food, binged occasionally, but always forced herself to vomit after eating so she would not get fat.

She had never forgotten the day of her twelfth birthday when her mother looked at her with disgust and said, "I didn't have time to bake you a birthday cake, but you don't need it anyway. You're already fat enough!" She had never thought she was fat until that day, but every day since, she looked at herself in the mirror and saw a girl who looked about thirty pounds heavier than she actually was. Her image of herself was distorted through the mean and unloving things her mother repeatedly said to her.

Jamie's grades in school were not very good and she did not feel she was "college material," so when she graduated from high school she got a job stocking shelves and bagging groceries at a local grocery store. She would never make enough money to move away from home on her own, but she was able to buy her clothes, her booze, and a few drugs when she wanted to really zone out. Most of the rest of the time, she avoided being at home by sitting at the coffee shop or walking around the neighborhood and wondering what all the other families who lived there were like. She didn't have any real friends—at least not people she trusted or felt she could count on. The people in her life were takers, not givers, and she was afraid of most of them.

One day she finally felt brave enough to go inside the church while the other people were crowding in. She merged into the crowd, partly hoping she wouldn't be noticed, but partly desperate for someone to welcome her and say, "We are so glad you're here today." She did notice people staring at her and some of them were even whispering, but nobody seemed friendly. Jamie dressed a bit wild for most people's taste and her hair was about three different colors. It was basically black, with red and blonde streaks. She wore baggy jeans and a baggy shirt. She didn't do it for comfort; she was trying to hide what she thought was her overweight body. She had on flip-flops, which, of course, nobody wore to church—at least not to that church!

Jamie sat in the last row and basically didn't understand anything that was going on. People kept standing up and reading things out of a book that was neatly placed in a rack on the back of the pew in front of them; then they sat down again. There was some singing, organ playing, and praying, and a collection plate was passed around and some people put money into it. A man who looked rather unhappy and a bit angry delivered a twenty-minute sermon, which she really didn't understand. She thought he was the pastor, but couldn't be sure. Finally, the service seemed to be coming to an end because they all stood up again and sang one more song.

She thought perhaps someone would say something to her on the way out. Surely, somebody would say something! The pastor stood by the door shaking hands with people as they filed out of the church and when Jamie reached him he didn't smile or even make eye contact with her. She could tell he was simply doing his duty and couldn't wait for it to be over.

As she walked down the steps, she realized that a woman appeared to be waiting for her at the bottom of the steps. She grew a little excited thinking someone had noticed her after all. The woman had noticed her all right, but she noticed everything she thought was wrong about the way Jamie looked, so she said, "My name is Margaret Brown. What is your name?" Jamie responded with her name and Margaret went on to say, "You are always welcome here, but I thought I would help you by letting you know that we dress up when we come to church here at Holiness Tabernacle. No jeans, no flip-flops, and you might want to consider a hairstyle that draws less attention. You know, sweetie, that Jesus teaches us to be humble and not draw attention to ourselves." She smirked at Jamie and repeated, "You are welcome anytime."

Jamie couldn't go to the coffee shop that day; she had to go somewhere and be alone to cry. She felt that now God had rejected her, too, and she spent the remainder of the day contemplating suicide. She was at the bottom of the pit and felt she had no reason at all to live.

These names have been fictionalized. But the world is filled with Jamies and Holiness Tabernacles and religious women like Mrs. Brown. It is filled with Christians who file in and out of churches each week. Many of them dread going and can't wait until the service is over. They are critical, judgmental, and very exclusive!

God Loves Everybody the Same

Jesus probably wasn't at Holiness Tabernacle the day Jamie went because He would not have felt comfortable there either. But had He been there, He would have been watching for the Jamies who might come that day. He would have either taken a seat beside her or walked her closer to the front to sit with Him, and He would have asked if she was a visitor. When He discovered she was a first-time visitor, He would have offered to explain anything she didn't understand. He would have smiled at her every time she looked at Him and, knowing Him, He would have complimented her on her unique hairstyle because He happens to like variety! He would have even invited her across the street to have coffee with the group He usually went with and by the time Jamie left she would have been looking forward to returning the next week. But of course Jesus wasn't there that day because none of the people acted as He would act. Nobody represented Him properly; and nobody was imitating God.

No Respecter of Persons

The Bible says in several places that God is not a respecter of persons (see Acts 10:34, Rom. 2:11, Eph. 6:9). In other words, He does not treat some people better than others because of the way they dress, their levels of income, the positions they hold, or who they know. He not only treats everyone the same, it seems He goes out of His way to treat those who are hurting especially well. God gave Moses many instructions to deliver to the Israelites concerning how to treat the strangers in their midst and His primary directive was always basically, "Make them feel comfortable and at ease and be friendly with them. Do not oppress them in any way" (see Exod. 22:21, Exod. 23:9, Lev. 19:33). The Apostle Peter said this:

> Practice hospitality to one another (those of the
> household of faith) [Be hospitable, be a lover of
> strangers, with brotherly affection for the unknown
> guests, the foreigners, the poor, and all others who
> come your way who are of Christ's body]. And [in each
> instance] do it ungrudgingly (cordially and graciously,
> without complaining but as representing Him).
> *1 Peter 4:9*

Before you rush past this part take an inventory of how friendly you are with people you don't know and especially those who are entirely different from you. Some people are just naturally friendly and outgoing in temperament, but those of us who didn't seem to get the "friendly gene" need to just make a decision to do it because the Bible says to do it.

The apostle James admonished the church not to pay special attention to people who wore splendid clothes to the synagogue or to give them preferable seats when they came in. He said that if people acted in these ways and wanted special treatment, they were discriminating and they had wrong motives. He said that we were not even to attempt to practice the faith of our Lord Jesus Christ together with snobbery (see James 2:1–4). In other words we are to treat all people as being worthy of respect.

Jesus put an end to distinction between people and said that we are all one in Him (see Gal. 3:28). We simply need to see valuable people, not black, red, or white people, not the labels in their clothes, hairstyles, the cars they drive, their professions or titles—just people for whom Jesus died.

A Lesson from the Coffee Shop

I believe we all need to consider our circles of inclusion and make them broader. We need to make them wide enough to include all kinds of people. I was recently with Paul Scanlon, a pastor in Birmingham, England, and we were having coffee in a coffee shop with several people. I remember looking at the hairstyle of the girl who was waiting on us and, to be honest, it was the absolutely strangest thing I had ever seen. Her head was shaved except for what is called a Mohawk going down the middle, and it was black, blue, red, and white. She also had her nose, her tongue, her lip, and several places on her ears pierced. I remember feeling a bit uncomfortable because she was not anything like I am. We were so different that I couldn't even think of anything to say that she might relate to. I just wanted to order my coffee and try not to stare.

Paul, on the other hand, started a conversation with her and the first thing he said was, "I like your hair. How do you get it to stand up like that?" He continued the discussion with her and the air that had felt tight suddenly relaxed. Soon we were all at ease and I could feel that we were all starting to join in their conversation and include her in our circle. I learned a huge lesson that day—that I am not as "modern" as I might like to think I am. I still have some stinking religious thinking that needs to be dealt with and I need to get to a new level of making all people, including those who are a bit different, feel comfortable and included.

Perhaps to the girl in the coffee shop, I was the one who was unusual and different. Why do we always set ourselves as the standard for what is acceptable and assume that anyone who is different must have a problem? What is the right hairstyle, or clothing style? One day I started thinking about what Moses must have looked like when he returned from Mount Sinai, where he spent forty days and nights receiving The Ten Commandments from God. I bet his hair was messed up; his beard seriously needed to be trimmed; and his robe and sandals were a bit dirty.

I know that John the Baptist was a bit strange. He lived in the desert alone and wore animal skins and ate honey and locusts. When he did come out, he yelled loudly, "Repent you sinners, for the Kingdom of God is at hand!"

The Bible teaches that we should be careful how we treat strangers because we might be entertaining angels without knowing it (see Heb. 13:2). It says we should be kind, cordial, friendly, and gracious to them and share the comforts of our homes. Most people in society today don't even speak to strangers, let alone be friendly.

I know, I know; you are probably saying, "Joyce, we live in a different world today! You never know who you are talking to!" I realize you must use wisdom, but don't let fear make you unfriendly and cold. Surely you can look for the new person at church, work, school, or in the neighborhood and say hello!

Surely you can talk to the elderly woman sitting in the doctor's office while you wait to be called for your appointment. She seems so lonely; why not give her ten minutes of your undivided attention and just let her tell you all about herself. You'll probably never see her again, but she will remember you. Oh, and by the way, God will appreciate what you did for her. Yes, it was a little thing, but you included her!

Following this chapter you will read a guest chapter from Paul Scanlon, who tells the story of his experience trying to take his church from being a dead, religious one to a church experiencing revival and filled with love. His story can teach us a lot and provoke us to ask ourselves some hard-to-answer questions. If true revival came to your church, would you really be excited or would you leave because many of the people would be like Jamie was or much worse? They might come from the shelters and not smell good, or they could reek of alcohol or other unpleasant things. The hurting people in the world don't always make the best presentation or smell nice. Sometimes they do, but not always and we must stop judging by the cover and be willing to read the book. Be willing to look beyond how people appear and find out what they are all about.

Step Outside Your Comfort Zone

Going out of your comfort zone to make someone else feel comfortable is one way to show the love of God to people. Many Christians love praying for revival; they even cry as they pray

Going out of your comfort zone to make someone else feel comfortable is one way to show the love of God to people.

about all the "lost souls in the world" but to be honest, some of those same people would leave if a revival actually came to their church because it would mess with their normal lifestyle and they wouldn't like it.

I recently preached in a church where all the wheelchair patients from local nursing homes sit along the front of the church. Being the speaker, I was put in the front row, but the wheelchairs were lined up in front of the front row. The man who sat directly in front of me smelled really bad, and I have a really weak stomach when it comes to bad smells. (When our children were small, I got Dave to change the smelly diapers anytime he was home.)

Sitting there, I recognized God's sense of humor; He had me right where He wanted me.... I was getting ready to get up and preach a message to the church about love and inclusion! I had to do a lot of praying while I was waiting to speak, and I must have looked very spiritual because I kept my nose up in the air as much as possible, so it probably seemed as if I was looking up to heaven. I knew God had arranged for me to sit there and that in fact I *needed* to be there. It was very good for me to experience having to do what I was getting ready to tell others to be willing to do. We don't always have to be comfortable everywhere we go! That man probably had nobody to bathe him regularly and couldn't do anything about the way he smelled. By the way, that might be a good ministry for somebody who is looking for one. Go to a local nursing home and volunteer to help keep the patients clean!

Jamie Tries Again

As we close this chapter, let me finish sharing Jamie's story with you. After her sad experience with church, she vowed never to do that again (go to church, that is). She went to work on Monday, obviously depressed, when one of her co-workers noticed and asked her what was wrong. Jamie normally kept everything to herself, but she was so hurt she started to cry. Her co-worker, Samantha, asked the manager if they could take their break early and she took Jamie to the employee lounge to try to help her feel better. After Jamie poured out her heart to Samantha, even telling her about her awful experience at trying church, Samantha invited her to come to her house for dinner so they could continue talking. That evening proved to be life changing for Jamie.

Samantha was a real Christian—I mean the kind who really cares and wants to help. She began to meet with Jamie twice a week and started not only caring for her, but gradually teaching her about Jesus and how much He loved her. After about three months, Samantha asked Jamie if she would try church one more time and attend with her that Sunday. Jamie was not very excited, but felt she owed it to Samantha after all the time she spent with her.

Jamie's visit to Resurrection Church was quite different from her experience at the previous church. She was greeted warmly and given special seating close to the front because she was a guest. Everything about the service seemed to be just for her. She understood it all because it related to real life. The songs they sang had meaning and each one made her feel better. She was invited for coffee after the service this time and ended up meeting several people who eventually became her closest friends. In this church, there were lots of people of all ages and cultures. Some wore suits and ties, while others wore jeans and T-shirts. Everybody was free to be themselves.

Jamie gave her life to Jesus and she wouldn't miss church now. She is married, has two children, and her entire family is part of the inner-city outreach, which ministers to people living on the street. Jamie likes doing that because she realizes she could easily have been among them!

Wouldn't it have been tragic if Jamie had ended her life as she thought of doing on that day she had such a sad church experience? I hate it when people try church thinking they have tried God, and then give up on Him because the church they tried did not represent Him properly. Let's make sure we include all kinds of people in our circle. Don't ever exclude anyone because they are not like you. We all have people we consider our closest friends and that is not wrong, even Jesus had three of the twelve disciples with whom He spent more time with than He spent with others. But He never slighted anyone or made them feel anything less than totally valuable.

LOVE REVOLUTIONARY
Pastor Paul Scanlon

The local church is the best idea God ever had! We are God's "pay it forward" community, we are His overflow, His expression, His smile, and His address in town. Sadly, many churches don't realize this, and as a result, millions within reach of God's house die in the sorrow of their own houses, never recognizing Jesus through the disguise of religion and irrelevancy many churches wear.

Crossing Over

Ten years ago, our church went through an extreme makeover and the pain was excruciating. We call it our "crossing over," and the story of that process has now become a book by the same name, which journals our story in detail. The average church size in the United Kingdom, where we are located, is twenty people, and 98 percent of the population not only does not attend church but is actually "anti-church." So by British standards we were a fairly large church of more than 450 people at that time, based in a building that was almost paid for. We were close, happy, and prosperous. We enjoyed great preaching and were a very gifted church musically and creatively. Yet despite all of this, something huge was missing. Something deeply fundamental was absent, but nobody seemed to notice.

We were trapped in what seemed like an endless cycle of looking after what could only be described as "high-maintenance, overfed, and under-exercised Christians." High-maintenance

Christians are one of the devil's best-kept secrets in his plan to neutralize the church. These are some of the nicest people you will ever meet, and therein lies the problem! None of these people were unhappy or had "bad hearts" or poor attitudes. Looking back, I would have preferred that because it would have made the need for our reinvention easier to sell.

Pastors all over the world are at a loss to describe what's missing in their churches and ministries, and they don't want to appear restless or negative by saying so, like the boy in the story *The Emperor's New Clothes* who pointed out what was so obvious to everyone around the emperor: he didn't have any clothes on.

When everyone is so happy, loving, friendly, and blessed, who wants to announce that we are dying? But in late 1998 I became that boy, and for the first time in twenty years, I had to point at our church and say, "We are naked, comfortable, intense, safe, and irrelevant"—and that included me. It was not easy for us to see this because, like many churches, we had a theology and language about reaching the lost but were not actually reaching anyone. We prayed for the lost, preached and sang about the lost, we even wept over the lost, but no lost were being rescued. We had become an inward-looking religious club, and in our comfort and blessing had lost sight of God's heart for others who were still missing and hurting.

In January 1999, I preached a message entitled, "We Are Leaving the 99 in '99," referring to Jesus, who described Himself as a shepherd who leaves the majority—the 99—for the one still lost. I explained this meant those already in the church could no longer be our first priority, but that our priority must become others. This was when I discovered that hell hath no fury like a neglected Christian! I was stunned by the reaction of good, Spirit-filled people who, when push came to shove, could not stomach the idea of our beautiful church being trashed by an influx of dirty sinners.

In my continued efforts to get our comfortable and exclusive members club back into the life-saving business, I launched a bus ministry in 1999. How God told me to do this is a story in itself. But suffice to say it was unusual enough to convince me that it was a "God idea," because the last thing I needed was just a good idea.

Well, within weeks we were busing in hundreds of those dirty sinners. These unchurched, often rough, rude, and unpredictable people ruined our beautiful club. They were referred to as the "bus people" by our respectable members, who viewed them as a threat to our safety and stability. Every day I received unpleasant, often nasty and threatening letters and phone calls from people I loved, and who I'm sure loved me, but who just didn't get it. The kids who came on the buses were accused of ruining our Sunday school, and their parents were accused of ruining the main service, usually by smoking, swearing, and worst of all, wait for it, actually daring to sit where our long-standing members usually sat.

Wave after wave of leaders came to see me, urging and persuading me to stop, but it was too late. God's heart for the lost had found my heart and I was becoming completely unreasonable. For almost two years I endured the greatest loneliness, isolation, and personal attack I had ever experienced. And what made it all the more difficult to endure was that it was all friendly fire from people who had clearly forgotten that they too had once been drowning at sea and yet someone had come looking for them.

When all of this failed to dissuade me, the "prophecy crowd" arrived. These were the so-called prophetic types among us. They started to make appointments to see me, often coming in groups, to share what God had told them to tell me. Their message amounted to this: "If you don't stop this, our church will split, you and your family will suffer, leaders will leave, finances will drop, and our testimony in the country will be damaged." But to me, just because the price was going to be high did not mean that God was saying, "Don't do it." If He was sending messages He was simply saying that if I did do it, here was a heads-up about the cost. My reply could only be that I agreed, because most of that was already happening. Many were leaving, and without their giving we were dropping tens of thousands of dollars a month. We were slowly growing back those who were leaving but with poor people—and the poor not only have no money but are expensive to reach and expensive to sustain.

Getting the local church to reach their communities is still for me the greatest battle we face across the church in the world today. And if that's true, the biggest shaking for the church is still to come. Maybe as pastors we will have to be willing to lose hundreds to gain thousands and even thousands to gain millions.

I love the local church. I've been in the same one for more than thirty years, twenty-six of those in full-time ministry there. But as much as I love the church, I refuse to die in the comfort of soft Christianity. I have determined to live full and die empty. I cannot do that within the four walls of the local church, and neither can you.

In the early days of Jesus' ministry, He went to a town called Capernaum. The people loved Him; they were amazed by His teaching and His power over demons and sickness. They loved

Him so much that on the day He was about to leave town, Luke tells us that the people came to Him and tried to keep Him from leaving (see Luke 4:42).

His response to their no-doubt persuasive attempts to keep Him is both stunning and profound. Stunning in its simplicity, and profound because of the insight it gives into His priorities and driving force. Jesus looked into the eyes of all those blessed people and simply said, "I can't stay here with you any longer because I was sent to reach other people in other places and I must go and preach the good news to them also. Did you get that? I was sent to reach others, others, others!" (see Luke 4:43). It's all about others.

If you could cut God, He would bleed others. But if we could cut the church, sadly, we would bleed ourselves. We bleed our blessing, our comfort, and our happiness. Of course, there are exceptions to this, but the exceptions are far too rare to believe we are tipping the balance in favor of others. For generations, the church, like the people of Capernaum, has been trying to keep Jesus to itself, and for generations Jesus has been trying to leave comfortable Christianity to continue reaching others. This fundamental misunderstanding about what matters most to God is at the heart of the church's failure to impact a hurting world.

We are blessed to be a blessing; we are saved to seek and save others. We are healed to heal, forgiven to forgive, and we are loved to join God's great Love Revolution. It is not about me, us, ours, me, or mine. It has always been about others.

The apostle Paul said that even the comfort we receive from God does not belong to us alone: "Praise be to the God and Father of our Lord Jesus Christ, the Father of compassion and the God of all comfort, who comforts us in all our troubles, so that we can comfort those in any trouble with the comfort we ourselves have received from God. For just as the sufferings of Christ flow over into our lives, so also through Christ our comfort overflows" to *others* (2 Cor. 1:3–5 NIV).

Even our troubles don't belong to us exclusively; within them is the seed of another person's comfort, hope, and inspiration. My blessing is not my blessing; my mercy is not my mercy; my grace not my grace; and ultimately, my life not my life. It all belongs to others, and those others were once you and me.

Watching good people you love and with whom you've "done life" for twenty years leave the church is extremely painful. The pain of sometimes having to separate from those we thought we would grow old with is also a birth pain. Of course, at the time it is difficult to see anything good in something so bad, but whatever we can't leave is where we stop, and if we stop we will never know what could have been. God never makes reluctant people move on; we have to decide to move on. In every sorrow there's a seed, and mine was the seed of the new church that we were becoming, a life-saving church.

In late 1998, I had led the church into the biggest building project we, and maybe any church in our country in recent history, had ever attempted, a two-thousand-seat auditorium. I did this out of my growing conviction that if I built it, the lost would come. I only wish they had come sooner, because by the time we held our first service in the new building our church had shrunk down to about 300 people. I have to tell you that no matter how creative you may be with chairs, there's only so much space you can put between them without people feeling that they're not in the same room! Three hundred in a two-thousand-seater looked a mess, especially when we had our existing six-hundred-seat facility just across the parking lot.

This was January 2000, and on that day God gave me a word from the story of Isaac re-digging his father's wells (see Gen. 26). Isaac moved on from the first two wells he dug because the Philistines filled them in. He named them *Esek* and *Sitnah*, meaning "contention" and "resistance." He moved on and dug a third well, but this time no one quarreled or filled it in. He named this third well *Rehoboth*, meaning "room," saying, "Now God has made room for me." On that first Sunday morning service in our two-thousand-seat auditorium, I looked at three hundred worn-out, pretty beat-up people and preached a message called, "Well Number Three Is Gonna Be a Gusher." After almost two years of contention and resistance, I believed the time for our Rehoboth had come. Now, years later, with a church of thousands, our Rehoboth has truly come.

During the final hours of Jesus' life, standing in Pilate's court, He was given the chance of freedom by being offered to the crowd along with a man named Barabbas. It was customary at the feast to release a prisoner whom the people requested. Barabbas was a convicted murderer and a rebel leader. Jesus hadn't been convicted of anything, and all He had ever done was help people. Yet, amazingly, the crowd shouted for Barabbas to be released and for Jesus to be crucified. The truth is the world would always prefer a rebel over a revolutionary. The dictionary defines a rebel as "someone who is resistant or defiant against a government or a ruler." But a revolutionary is "someone who overthrows a government or social order in favor of a new system."

This book is about a Love Revolution, not a love rebellion. We are not rebelling against the world; we are seeking to revolutionize it. God so loved the world that He sent us an alternative, not an ultimatum. Our leader, Jesus Christ, is a revolutionary, not a rebel; He overcomes by replacing, not condemning. This becomes our challenge. If the church is to love the world, we must find new ways of loving the unlovely and including the excluded without being judgmental. We must live "behind enemy lines," not as a resistance movement, but as a replacement movement. We are God's alternative society.

While traveling through an airport in the United States recently, I noticed an older lady with a cane, struggling to place her belongings on the security screening belt. The security agent was stern with her and although seeing her stressed and struggling, did nothing to help her. I instinctively started grabbing her stuff and loading it onto the conveyer belt. On the other side, I waited with her to help retrieve everything from the belt. I will never forget how she looked at me and with a smile of relief said, "Thank you so much; your kindness compensated for that man's unkindness." That lady put into words my deepest conviction about the church: the church is God's compensation factor for a hurting world.

To compensate is "to give back, to reduce or balance out the bad effect of loss, suffering or injury by exerting an opposite force or effect." We are God's opposite effect; we balance out the pain and suffering in our communities. As ambassadors and merchants of love and hope, we bring a smile to the face of a stressed and struggling world. Compensation doesn't change what happened, but it can reduce the effect of what happened. A Love Revolution is part of God's great compensation plan for a world that has forgotten how to smile.

Our native environment is not the church; it's the world—not the comfortable club but the dangerous ocean. We were born to thrive in the adversity and hostility of a broken world. Like fish, which do better in water, we do better among a lost world because, like fish, we were designed to always stay in that native environment. Remove a fish from the water and it dies. Remove a flower from the soil and it dies. Remove the church from the world and we die. Fish don't ever feel wet because water is their home, and yet many Christians have a huge allergic reaction to their native environment. We are like fish toweling ourselves dry on the beach! A ridiculous image, I know, but a graphic and appropriate one nonetheless.

The Bible often portrays the church in a hostile environment. We are described as salt in a rotten world, light in darkness, sheep amongst wolves, foreigners and aliens away from our country. We were designed to thrive in hostility. We are the church, the only part of heaven built to prosper in a world poisoned by hell. We are God's revolutionary army sent to start a Love Revolution—and that revolution has to start in you and me today!

CHAPTER
9

Make People Feel Valuable

So let us then definitely aim for and eagerly pursue
what makes for harmony and for mutual upbuilding
(edification and development) of one another.

Romans 14:19

One of the easiest ways to help fuel a Love Revolution is to decide to make others feel valuable. Mother Teresa said, "Being unwanted, unloved, uncared for, forgotten by everybody, I think that is a much greater hunger, a much greater poverty than the person who has nothing to eat," and I have discovered that most people we meet or come into contact with in our everyday lives do not have a sense of their infinite value as children of God. I think the devil works very hard to make people feel devalued and worthless, but we can neutralize the effect of his lies and insinuations by building people up, encouraging, and edifying them. One way to do this is with a sincere compliment, which is one of the most valuable gifts in this world.

One of the easiest ways to help fuel a Love Revolution is to decide to make others feel valuable.

Most people are quick to compare themselves with others, and in doing so, they often fail to see their own abilities and worth. Making another person feel valuable isn't expensive and doesn't have to be time consuming. All we need to do is get ourselves off of our minds long enough to think about someone else and then find something encouraging to say. Making people feel valuable won't cost any money, but it gives them something worth more than anything money can buy. Offering a sincere compliment may seem like a small thing, but it gives tremendous strength.

I believe in having goals, and as I was working with God to develop good habits in the area of encouraging others I challenged myself to compliment at least three people each day. I recommend that you do something similar to help you become an aggressive encourager.

Don't Forget the Forgotten

People often feel lonely and forgotten. They may feel they work very hard but that nobody notices or cares. I remember a woman who told me she had felt invisible for most of her life. I remember the pain on her face as she recalled the way her parents basically ignored her. She felt isolated and terribly alone, which made her feel unwanted. Her parents were young when she was born; they were not ready to have a child and they were very selfish and self-centered. They gave her no affection or emotional support at all. She said she spent most of her childhood and teenage years alone in her room, reading.

This woman's description of her childhood and her feeling invisible was so sad, and it made me wonder how often I have made people feel invisible simply because I was so focused on what I was doing or the goal I was trying to accomplish that I did not even take the time to acknowledge their presence. I am a type A personality who is very focused and determined to reach my goals in life. I accomplish a lot, but have had to learn not to wound other people in the process. Nobody succeeds without the help of a lot of other dedicated people and failing to show them appreciation and give credit where it is due is a terrible tragedy and a type of behavior God is not pleased with.

Simple Things Can Be Great Things

God speaks frequently in the Bible of our responsibility to the oppressed, widows, orphans, fatherless, and foreigners. He mentions those who are lonely and those who feel neglected, forgotten, and devalued. He cares deeply for the oppressed and the hungry. People can be hungry in many ways. They may have plenty of food to eat but be starving for encouragement or some word that makes them feel valuable. God lifts up those who are bowed down with sorrow, He protects the stranger and He upholds the fatherless and the widow (see Ps. 146:7–9). How does He do this? He works through people! He needs committed, submitted, dedicated people who live to make others feel valuable. Mother Teresa gave her life to make the outcasts feel loved and valuable. The things she did were simple things, they were usually little things, yet they were great things. She said, "Do not think that love, in order to be genuine, has to be extraordinary. What we need is to love without getting tired."

We're Adopted

A Scripture that has encouraged me greatly is Psalm 27:10: "Although my father and my mother have forsaken me, yet the Lord will take me up [adopt me as His child]."

My mother was deeply afraid of my father, so she was unable to rescue me from the various kinds of abuse he perpetrated against me. I felt very alone, forgotten, and abandoned in my nightmare. I finally decided that nobody was going to help me, so I proceeded to "survive" my circumstances until I could escape them. I have come to understand that multitudes of people that we encounter daily are just trying to survive until someone rescues them—and that someone could be you or me.

The Bible says that in God's love, "He chose us [actually picked us out for Himself as His own] in Christ before the foundation of the world" (Eph. 1:4). He planned in love for us to be adopted as His own children. Those beautiful words brought a great deal of healing to my wounded soul. God adopts the forsaken and the lonely and He lifts them up and gives them value. He works through His Word, through the Holy Spirit, and through Spirit-led people who live to help others.

Mother Teresa felt that each person she met was "Jesus in disguise." Just try to imagine how much differently we would treat people if we really looked at them the way she did. Jesus said that if we do good or bad to even "the least" of people, we do it to Him (see Matt. 25:45). In other words, He takes our treatment of others personally. If someone insulted, slighted, ignored, or devalued one of my children, I would take it as a personal insult, so why is it so hard to understand that God feels the same way? Let us all strive to build people up, to make everyone we encounter feel better, and to add value to their lives.

Start with a Smile

A smile is the beginning of love. It signifies acceptance and approval. We should learn to smile at everyone and when we do, not only will they feel better, we will feel better too.

I am usually deep in thought and because of that I can look rather intense. I also carry a lot of responsibility and, if I am not careful, that can make me appear somber. I am learning to take the time to smile at people, ask how they are, and find something friendly to say to them. Surely if we are too busy to be friendly then we are out of balance and headed for relational disaster. Relationships are a large part of life and actually I have found the Bible to be a book about relationships. It is about our relationships with God, with ourselves, and with other people.

It is amazing how a smile and a friendly greeting put people at ease. These are two of many ways we can give to others everywhere we go. You might be thinking, *Well, that is just not me. I am more reserved and private. I just prefer not to get involved with people that much, especially people I don't know.* If you feel that way, I understand because I was exactly the same way until I

kept seeing what the Bible says about encouragement, edification, exhortation, and making people feel valuable. I have
learned that the fact that I may not be naturally gifted in an
area doesn't mean I can't learn how to do it.

For years, I excused myself from being friendly by saying,
"That just isn't me; I am more of a loner," but I realized that
"loner" is not listed as a gift in the Bible. Thinking of ourselves
as "loners" is simply an excuse to avoid the often messy business of being vulnerable. After all, we think, *How will I feel if I
smile at people and they don't smile back?* I will feel rejected, and
that never feels good. Most of us spend more time in life trying
to avoid rejection than we do trying to develop good, healthy
relationships. What if I try to make friendly conversation with
a stranger while waiting at the doctor's office and it is evident
he or she wants to be left alone? Suddenly I am now embarrassed and feeling odd, so rather than "chance it," I may remain
isolated for my own protection. When this happens, we are
missing the opportunity to touch people with the love of God
through a smile or friendly word. When we give our smiles, we
can make someone else smile and that is one of the best gifts we
can give.

Being part of a Love Revolution will require effort and practice. It will demand that we be willing to change some of our
ways and begin asking God to show us His ways. Can you
really imagine Jesus frowning and being unfriendly or ignoring
people just so He did not feel rejected or merely because He was
too busy doing His own thing to even notice them? Of course
we know Jesus could never act that way and we should decide
that we will not either. Start smiling more, you can even try
smiling when you are alone and you will see that it makes you

feel lighter and happier. The apostle Paul told those to whom he ministered to greet one another with a holy kiss (see Rom. 16:16), which was customary in their day. I am only asking for a smile!

Don't Worry If It Doesn't Come Naturally

At the end of this chapter, you will read a contribution to this book from John Maxwell, an international speaker and author on the subject of leadership and a friend of ours. Within a few minutes of being in John's presence, everyone feels amazingly valuable. He and I have talked about his great ability in this area and he readily admits that his father affected him the same way. Not only did John have a good example as he was growing up, he also has the gift (talent, ability) of encouragement given to him from God.

The Bible speaks of the gift of encouragement (see Rom. 12:8) and says people who have been given that gift should embrace it with zeal and cheerful, joyful eagerness. Just as I have a gift of communication that enables me to speak effectively without much effort, some people have the gift of encouragement. They encourage others without much effort at all; it comes naturally for them. Although some might devalue the gift of encouragement, I think it is one of the most needed gifts in the world.

These people are wonderful to know or be around, but once again, I urge you not to discount yourself just because encouraging others does not come naturally to you. I have the gift of giving and can remember as a small child loving to make plans to give someone a present that would make him or her happy.

Everyone may not have the spiritual gift of giving (which is also listed in Romans 12, along with being able to encourage others), but everyone is instructed to give and to do so on purpose.

Go Ahead and Laugh

Most of us have heard at least something about the value of laughter to our physical and psychological health. Smiling is the doorway to laughter, which is something we need to do frequently and on purpose.

The Bible says that a merry heart does good like a medicine (see Prov. 17:22). One of the amazing things I have noticed about my teaching ministry is that I am very funny. I call it amazing, because in what I would call "normal life," that would not be the way people would describe me. I have realized that since it is the Holy Spirit speaking through me He obviously knows the value of humor and the healing effect it brings.

God wants us to laugh, and He wants us to make other people laugh. That does not mean we should all become jesters or laugh at inappropriate times, but we can certainly aid one another in taking a more lighthearted approach to life. We would all be much better off if we would learn to laugh at ourselves sometimes instead of taking ourselves so seriously.

The last three times I have worn white pants, I have spilled coffee on myself. I can either think I am a klutz who cannot hold on to anything and begin to devalue myself or I can make a joke out of it and try harder to stay clean next time. For years, I have listened to people downgrade themselves verbally for every mistake they make and I believe that grieves God. If we

know our value in Christ we should *never* say things about ourselves that devalue what God has created.

Why not make a habit of helping people to see that we all
make silly mistakes and we can choose to laugh or to get upset
about them? Give people permission to not be perfect! The
world is filled with pressure to perform and excel, but when
don't we need a word of kindness that lets us know we are still
accepted and valuable.

When you are with people who make mistakes, try immediately reminding them of the strengths they have or of something
amazing you have seen them do recently. My two daughters are
both wonderful, dedicated mothers. When they are feeling bad
about something they have not done correctly, I remind them
that they are great moms and emphasize how important that is.
We should not take anything that people do well for granted. The
devil works overtime trying to make people feel like a failure and
we should work equally hard to make them feel like a success.

Nothing turns a bad situation around faster than laughter. We
stifle the "little child" in us far too early in life. Children don't
seem to get so upset about dropping something, messing up their
clothes, tripping and falling, or making a mistake. They usually
find a way to keep laughing and having fun as long as adults will
let them. Jesus said that we could not enter the wonderful life
God promises unless we come as little children (see Luke 18:17),
so I highly recommend that we help one another in this area.

I love to be around people who do not pressure me to be perfect. God loves us unconditionally and that means He accepts
us the way we are and then helps us to be all we can be. Smiling
is a sign of acceptance. Helping people laugh at themselves is a
way of saying, "I accept you, faults and all."

Bearing with one another's weaknesses is just one simple way of showing love. The apostle Paul had taught people to encourage and build up others and he frequently reminded them to keep doing it. "Therefore encourage (admonish, exhort) one another and edify (strengthen and build up) one another, just as you are doing" (1 Thess. 5:11). The Holy Spirit Himself is the One who lives in us and walks alongside us in life and comforts, encourages, and edifies us. He urges us to become all we can be. When we make mistakes, He does not condemn us; He urges us forward.

Lack of encouragement causes depression, despair, failure, and divorce, and it prevents people from reaching their potential in life. We all need to be encouraged and once again I want to press the point that simple encouragement is one of the primary ways we can fuel a Love Revolution in our society.

Accentuate the Positive

God began showing me that one way I could love my husband was by simply not mentioning little mistakes he made—things like not turning off the light in his closet or not replacing the toilet paper. Perhaps he forgot to do something I had asked him to do—such as taking my briefcase upstairs to my office so I would not have to carry it up the next morning while trying to balance my coffee. There are literally hundreds of little things we all do that tend to irritate one another, but we can choose to let them go and remember that we all make little mistakes and would rather people not keep reminding us of them.

If you really need to confront an issue then by all means do it, but most relationships that are torn apart end because someone makes a huge deal out of a little thing that was not really important after all. People are torn down and actually weakened each time they are reminded of something they did not do right. I spent a lot of years "mentioning" the things that irritated me in the hopes that people would stop doing them, but I found my comments only pressured them and made them uncomfortable in my presence. I have found prayer and accentuating the positive to be much more effective.

When we make a big deal out of people's strengths and the things they do right, they are motivated to overcome their weaknesses and faults. I was surprised to find what a huge challenge it was for me in the beginning of my quest to just not mention something that irritated me and totally let it go. I have now come to the place where I understand my irritation over little things is a bigger problem than the things themselves. Why is leaving a closet light on something that should irritate me? Do I ever leave lights on? Of course, I do.

I recently corrected Dave for sitting on the end of the bed I had already made and then walking off without fixing it. He looked at me, shocked, and called to my attention that I was actually the one who had been sitting on the bed; he wasn't! Amazing! I was so sure it was Dave that I totally forgot that *I* was the guilty party! This example shows how a faultfinding spirit can blind us to our own faults while urging us to accuse others.

Show love by accentuating the positive in people. Oddly enough, we don't have to try to find the negative things they do. Those seem to stick out like red flashing lights. But we have to look for the positive on purpose—or at least until we form new habits!

As I suggested earlier, start by having a goal of encouraging or complimenting three people every day without fail. At the end of the day, ask yourself who they were as a method of accountability. When three becomes natural increase your goal to six, then 10, and by then it will be natural for you to encourage everyone you contact in everyday life.

Your compliment does not have to be something major. Little things such as, "That color really looks good on you," "I like your hair that way," "Your shirt is nice," "You make me feel safe," "You work hard," "I appreciate you," or "I am glad you are my friend" are very effective and meaningful. As you give out and accentuate the positive, you will feel happier. So not only are you giving, you are receiving a benefit at the same time.

LOVE REVOLUTIONARY
John C. Maxwell

Encouragement Changes Everything

Encouragement is incredible. Its impact can be profound—nearly miraculous. A word of encouragement from a teacher to a child can change his life. A word of encouragement from a spouse can save a marriage. A word of encouragement from a leader can inspire a person to reach her potential. As Zig Ziglar says, "You never know when a moment and a few sincere words can have an impact on a life." To encourage people is to help them gain courage they might not otherwise possess—courage to face the day, to do what's right, to take risks, to make a difference. And the heart of encouragement is to communicate a person's value. When we help people feel valuable, capable, and motivated, we often get to see their lives change forever. And we sometimes get to see them go on to change the world.

If you are a parent, you have a responsibility to encourage members of your family. If you are an organizational leader, you can increase the effectiveness of your team dramatically in proportion to the amount of encouragement you give the people you lead. As a friend, you have the privilege of sharing encouraging words that may help someone persevere through a rough time or strive for greatness. As a Christian, you have the power to represent Jesus by loving others and lifting them up with an encouraging word.

Join the Club

Never underestimate the power of encouragement. In the 1920s, physician, consultant, and psychologist George W. Crane began teaching social psychology at Northwestern University in Chicago. Though he was new to teaching, he was an astute student of human nature, and he believed strongly in making the study of psychology practical to his students.

One of the first classes he taught contained evening students who were older than the average college student. The young men and women worked in the department stores, offices, and factories of Chicago by day and were trying to improve themselves by attending classes at night.

After class one evening a young woman named Lois, who had moved to Chicago from a small town in Wisconsin to take a civil service job, confided in Crane that she felt isolated and lonely.

"I don't know anybody, except a few girls at the office," she lamented. "At night I go to my room and write letters home. The only thing that keeps me living from day to day is the hope of receiving a letter from my friends in Wisconsin."

It was largely in response to Lois's problem that Crane came up with what he called the Compliment Club, which he announced to his class the following week. It was to be the first of several practical assignments he would give his students that term.

"You are to use your psychology every day either at home or at work or on the streetcars and buses," Crane told them. "For the first month, your written assignment will be the Compliment Club. Every day you are to pay an honest compliment to each of three different persons. You can increase that number if you

wish, but to qualify for a class grade, you must have complimented at least three people every day for thirty days...Then,
at the end of the thirty-day experiment, I want you to write a
theme or paper on your experiences," he continued. "Include
the changes you have noted in the people around you, as well
as your own altered outlook on life."[1]

Some of Crane's students resisted this assignment. Some
complained that they wouldn't know what to say. Others were
afraid of being rejected. And a few thought it would be dis-
honest to compliment someone they didn't like. "Suppose you
meet somebody you dislike?" one man asked. "Wouldn't it be
insincere to praise your enemy?"

"No, it is not insincerity when you compliment your enemy,"
Crane responded, "for the compliment is an honest statement
of praise for some objective trait or merit that deserves com-
mendation. You will find that nobody is entirely devoid of merit
or virtue...

"Your praise may buoy up the morale of lonely souls who are
almost ready to give up the struggle to do good deeds. You
never know when your casual compliment may catch a boy
or girl, or man or woman, at the critical point when he would
otherwise toss in the sponge."[2]

Crane's students discovered that their sincere compliments had a positive impact on the people around them, and
the experience made an even greater impact on the students
themselves. Lois blossomed into a real people person who
lit up a room when she entered it. Another student who was
ready to quit her job as a legal secretary because of an especially difficult boss began complimenting him, even though at
first she did so through clenched teeth. Eventually not only did

his surliness toward her change, but so did her exasperation with him. They wound up taking a genuine liking to each other and were married.

George Crane's Compliment Club probably sounds a little bit corny to us today. But the principles behind it are just as sound now as they were in the 1920s. The bottom line is that Crane was teaching what I call the Elevator Principle: We can lift people up or take people down in our relationships. He was trying to teach his students to be proactive. Crane said, "The world is starving for appreciation. It is hungry for compliments. But somebody must start the ball rolling by speaking first and saying a nice thing to his companion."[3] He embraced the sentiment of Benjamin Franklin, who believed, "As we must account for every idle word—so we must for every idle silence."

Five Things Every Encourager Needs to Know about People

You have tremendous power to affect the lives of people around you. Encouragement from you could be the difference-maker in someone's day, week, or even life, sending that person in a whole new direction.

It's difficult to encourage people if you don't know what encourages them. So become a student of people and learn what makes them tick. Know what lifts them up. To get you started, begin by embracing these five things I know about people:

1. Everybody wants to be somebody.
Every person wants to be affirmed. Every person wants to be loved. Every person wants to be well thought of. Everybody

wants to be somebody. That is true from the smallest of children to the oldest of adults.

How can you help other people to feel like they are somebody? By seeing them as a "10." I believe that for the most part, people respond to our expectations of them. If you think the best of them, they generally give you their best. If you treat people like a "10," they respond like a "10." If you treat someone like a "2," he responds like a "2." People want recognition and affirmation. It is a deep human desire, and we can help people become great simply by showing them how we believe in them.

2. Nobody cares how much you know until they know how much you care.

People don't want to know how smart we are. They don't want to know how spiritual we are. They don't want to know what degrees we possess or wealth we've amassed. The only thing they really want to know is whether we genuinely care about them. We need to show the love of God to others through our lives.

I learned this lesson from Katie Hutchison, my second-grade Sunday school teacher. She was incredible. She loved me and I knew it. When I was sick and missed church, she'd come visit me that week.

"Oh, Johnny, I missed you last Sunday in church," she'd say. "I wanted to see how you were doing." She'd give me a five-cent trinket that I thought was worth a million dollars, and say, "I hope you can come to Sunday school next Sunday because we missed you so much. In fact, when you come to class, I want to make sure I see you, so when I get up to teach, would you just raise your hand and wave to me?" (There were almost fifty kids in her class!) "Then I'll see you, and I'll smile, and I'll feel better and I'll teach better."

When Sunday came, I'd go whether I felt good or not. I'd wave. She'd smile, and nod, and teach. I knew how much she cared for me, and that made me feel like I could do anything.

3. Anybody in the body of Christ belongs to everybody in the body of Christ.

As Christians, too many people try to make it on their own. And they become indifferent to others and expect them to make it on their own too. But that's not how the body of Christ is meant to work.

When a Christian tries to go it alone, he's like the bricklayer in a humorous story I once came across. He needed to move about five hundred pounds of bricks from the top of a four-story building to the sidewalk below. The following is reputed to be his own words taken from an insurance claim form:

> It would have taken too long to carry the bricks down by hand, so I decided to put them in a barrel and lower them by a pulley which I had fastened to the top of the building. After tying the rope securely at ground level, I then went up to the top of the building, fastened the rope around the barrel, loaded it with bricks, and swung it over the sidewalk for the descent.
>
> Then I went down to the sidewalk and untied the rope, holding it securely to guide the barrel down slowly. But since I weigh only 140 pounds, the five-hundred-pound

load jerked me from the ground so fast that I didn't have time to think of letting go of the rope.

As I passed between the second and third floors, I met the barrel coming down. This accounts for the bruises and the lacerations on my upper body.

I held tightly to the rope until I reached the top, where my hand became jammed in the pulley. This accounts for my broken thumb.

At the same time, however, the barrel hit the sidewalk with a bang, and the bottom fell out. With the weight of the bricks gone, the barrel weighed only about forty pounds, thus my 140-pound body began a swift descent. I met the empty barrel coming up. This accounts for my broken ankle.

Slowed only slightly, I continued the descent and landed on the pile of bricks. This accounts for my sprained back and broken collarbone. At that point I lost my presence of mind completely, and I let go of the rope and the empty barrel came crashing down on me. This accounts for my head injuries.

And as for the last question on your insurance form— what would you do if the same situation arose again? Please be advised I am finished trying to do the job all by myself.[4]

In a spiritual sense, that's what happens when people remain disconnected from the body of Christ. God did not design any of us to go it alone. We were meant to encourage and help one another. As brothers and sisters, we need to take the journey together.

4. Anybody who encourages somebody influences a lot of bodies.

A lot of people have helped and encouraged me along the way in my life. I look back now at age sixty-one, and I am astounded by how generous and kind others have been.

One of the people who did that when I was a squirrely seventh grader was a man named Glen Leatherwood, another of my wonderful Sunday school teachers. We were an ornery group: always wiggling, squirming, talking, fighting—doing everything but listening. But we'd listen to Glen because he lived to love and encourage us.

One day his voice began to break, and every kid kind of turned around and looked up at Glen, and he looked at us, and tears were just streaming.

"Right after the class," he said, "I'd like to see Steve Benner, Phil Conrad, Junior Fowler, and John Maxwell just for a second. I've got something great to tell you."

After class when we met, he said, "Every Saturday night I pray for every boy in my seventh-grade class. Last night I felt God tell me that you four boys were going to be called into the ministry, and I wanted to be the first one to tell you. I also wanted to be the first to lay hands on you and pray for you."

Glen laid his hands on our heads and gave me what I have always considered to be my official ordination into the ministry. And he was right. All four of us become pastors in the ministry.

Many years later, I went to visit Glen, and I asked him how many people were in ministry from his Sunday school classes over the years. He said he wasn't sure, but he knew for sure there were thirty.

I wonder how many churches have benefited from the love

and encouragement he showed to bunches of seventh grad-
ers every year. How many lives have his encouraging words
impacted? I probably won't know until I get to heaven. But I
can tell you this: anybody who encourages somebody influences a lot of bodies.

5. God loves everybody.

Many Christians tend to be too choosy about who they help
and who they encourage. They look for people like themselves.
Some people even believe that they should help only other
individuals who believe what they believe and think as they do.
That's not the way it should be. It's certainly not the way Jesus
did it.

Years ago I came across a piece about someone who fell
into a pit and couldn't get out—and how others treated that
person:

> A subjective person came along and said, "I feel for you
> down there."
>
> An objective person came along and said, "Well, it's
> logical that someone would fall down there."
>
> A Pharisee said, "Only bad people fall into pits."
>
> A mathematician calculated how the individual fell into
> the pit.
>
> A news reporter wanted an exclusive story on the per-
> son in the pit.
>
> A fundamentalist said, "You deserve your pit."
>
> A Calvinist said, "If you'd been saved, you'd never fallen
> in that pit."
>
> An Armenian said, "You were saved and still fell in that pit."

A charismatic said, "Just confess that you're not in that pit."

A realist came along and said, "Now that's a pit."

A geologist told him to appreciate the rock strata in the pit.

An IRS worker asked if he was paying taxes on this pit.

The county inspector asked if he had a permit to dig the pit.

A self-pitying person said, "You haven't seen anything until you've seen my pit."

An optimist said, "Things could be worse."

A pessimist said, "Things will get worse."

Jesus, seeing the man, reached down and took him by the hand and lifted him out of the pit.

Jesus came to die for people. He was and is in the people business. And you and I need to be in the people business too. We should always keep in mind that God loves everybody, and we need to treat others the way Jesus would treat them. We need to encourage them to be who God created them to be.

I believe that deep down, everyone wants to become an encourager, and everyone who knows Jesus wants to be more like Jesus—even the most negative person. Why do I say that? Because I believe that we all want to be a positive influence on the lives of others. We want to add value to others, not take it away from them.

So please allow me to be your encourager. You can make a difference. You can add value to others. You can represent Jesus well and someday hear the words, "Well done, good and faithful servant." Everyone can become an encourager. You don't have to be rich. You don't have to be a genius. You don't have to have high charisma. And you don't have to have it all together. You just need to care about people and be willing to get started. You don't have to do anything big or spectacular. The little things you can do every day have the potential to have a much greater impact than you can imagine.

- Catch someone doing something right.
- Give someone a sincere compliment.
- Assist someone in need.
- Offer someone a shoulder to cry on.
- Celebrate with someone who succeeds.
- Give someone hope.

You can do this. Act now. And keep in mind this quote that I've always loved: "I expect to pass through this world but once. Any good therefore that I can do, or any kindness that I can show to any fellow creature, let me do it now. Let me not defer or neglect it, for I shall not pass this way again."[5]

CHAPTER

10

Aggressive Acts of Kindness

And let us consider and give attentive, continuous
care to watching over one another, studying how we
may stir up (stimulate and incite) to love and helpful
deeds and noble activities.

Hebrews 10:24

Have you ever sat with a spouse, family member, or friend and discussed ways you can be a blessing to others? I would venture to say that most of you haven't, and until about three years ago I hadn't either. Now, as I mentioned in chapter 6, I find such conversations to be fun and very helpful. We all get excited when we purposely think and talk about ways to help other people. There will be no Love Revolution if we don't do things on purpose that will help others. We must have goals and press toward meeting them.

Once I became determined to make loving others the theme of my life, I hungered for a variety of ways to show love. Love is not a theory or a mere talk; it is action (see 1 John 3:18). We can certainly love people with loving words that encourage and express how valuable we think they are, as I emphasized in the previous chapter, but we also need to use our resources of time, energy, possessions, and finances to love others.

You may be convinced you don't have anything to give. Maybe you are in debt, doing your best to pay your bills— and the thought of giving to others is almost irritating to you or perhaps makes you feel sad because you want to give, but don't see how you can. There are literally thousands of ways you can give and spread love if you will search for them aggressively.

Walk the Talk

I believe telling people what to do and failing to give them any information on how to do it is a huge mistake. Many people talk about love, but just talking doesn't necessarily leave people with any concrete ideas of how to show love in practical ways. I just finished skimming an entire book on love. It was 210 pages long and filled with teaching about how Jesus said the one new command we are to follow is to love one another as He has loved us and by that love the world would know Him (see John 13:34–35). But I did not find one practical idea or creative thought about *how* that would actually look in the life of an individual. The author repeatedly made the point that loving one another is the most important thing we can do, but I can honestly say that if his book was all the knowledge I had about love, I would not have any clue how to begin doing it. I think people want to do what is right, but they need someone to lead them by pointing them in the right direction.

Jesus not only talked about love, but remember that Acts 10:38 says He got up daily and went about doing good and healing all those who were harassed and oppressed by the devil. His disciples saw Him daily helping people, listening to them, or letting His plans be interrupted in order to help someone who came to Him with a need. They saw Him make sure they always had money set aside to help the poor. They also witnessed His being quick to forgive and showing patience with the weak. He was kind, humble, and encouraging, and never gave up on anybody. Jesus did not merely talk about loving people; He showed everyone around Him how to love. Our words are important, but our actions carry more weight than our words.

> Our words are important, but our actions carry more weight than our words.

Our Biggest Problem

The single biggest problem we have in Christianity is that we listen to people tell us what to do—and we even tell others what to do—and then we walk out of our church buildings or Bible studies and do nothing. It doesn't matter what we *think* we know. The proof of what we know is in what we do. Jesus said we would be known by our fruit (see Matt. 12:33), which means that people can tell who we really are on the inside by what we produce with our lives and by our attitude.

I must constantly ask myself, "What am I doing to actually show love?" We can be deceived by knowledge, according to the apostle Paul. We can become blinded by the pride of what we know to the point where we never see that we are not really practicing any of it. Paul told the Corinthians that mere knowledge causes people to be puffed up with pride, but love (affection and goodwill and benevolence) edifies and builds up and encourages people to grow to their full stature (see 1 Cor. 8:1). We should all make sure there is no gap between what we say and what we do. No wonder the world accuses many Christians of being hypocritical, for indeed they are.

I attended one church for many years that talked about missions once a year on "Missions Sunday." I don't remember ever hearing anything about reaching the poor and oppressed in our own city. Most of the sermons I heard were about doctrinal beliefs rather than the practical aspects of Christianity and how I should behave in my community. Solid doctrine is important, but understanding how to live my daily life is equally important. The church was filled with gossip, division, and people vying for position in the church. In many ways, we behaved no differently than the rest of the world; we simply went to church. I was finally asked to leave that church because I was too radical and enthusiastic about the supernatural gifts of God I had discovered were available to Christians. I had become an excited, enthusiastic Christian and was told I was just being emotional and needed to calm down.

I then went to another church where people were also enthusiastic about the things about which I felt strongly. They were heavily involved in witnessing to others about salvation through Jesus Christ. I was excited and deeply wanted to serve

God, so I organized a group of women and we went out armed with gospel tracts every Friday. We handed them to people as they exited the grocery store and put them on car windshields in the parking lot. Within a few weeks, we had distributed ten thousand little booklets containing the gospel message. I also hosted and taught a Bible study in my home each Tuesday evening.

I was growing in God and so excited about serving Him, but then the elders of the church called me into a meeting and said I was being rebellious because I organized the women to hand out tracts without getting their permission. They also informed Dave and me that he should be teaching the Bible study instead of me. That church finally dwindled to nothing and is now nonexistent simply because they tried to control people, and in doing so they often quenched the very gifts God had given.

For more years than I care to remember, I attended another church that taught good things, but to be honest, as I look back, I saw very little real love there. That church had minimal outreach and a budget for world outreach that was small and eventually eliminated. We also had leaders who were selfish, filled with pride, jealous, and even fearful of others' success; some were controlling and extremely immature. I get irritated every time I think that I wasted so much of my life being involved in something so self-contained. The Church in general and local churches specifically are called to outreach, not in-reach. The mission of the Church is to *be* a witness in communities, cities, nations, and the world (see Acts 1:8).

The Church is to function aggressively in the reality of love, which the Bible clearly defines as patience, kindness, humility, joy over the success of others, unselfishness, giving, always believing the best, being quick to forgive, showing mercy rather than judgment, benevolence, good deeds, and helping the poor, widows, orphans, the fatherless, the hungry, homeless, and the oppressed. Love lays down its own life for the good of others. In fact, love must be actively involved or it dies. It must flow and grow!

What Will You Do with Your Heart of Compassion?

First John 3:17 asks an important question: "But if anyone has this world's goods (resources for sustaining life) and sees his brother and fellow believer in need, yet closes his heart of compassion against him, how can the love of God live and remain in him?" In other words, this verse is saying that we can decide to open or close our hearts of compassion when we see a need, but if we decide to close them repeatedly, the love of God cannot stay alive and remain in us. The very nature of love requires that it be active because it is a living thing. God is love!

John made a startling and sobering comment when he said that "he who does not love has not become acquainted with God [does not and never did know Him], for God is love" (1 John 4:8). We can receive a quick education in what love is supposed to look like in everyday life by studying the steps of Jesus. Or, as one person said, "Perhaps we can learn more by studying the stops of Jesus." He always had time for people! He always cared! No matter where He was going, He stopped to help those in need.

Let's Get Practical

I have asked hundreds of people to share with me practical ways they believe we can show love. I have read books, searched the Internet, and been very aggressive on my own journey to find creative ways to incorporate this theme of loving people into my everyday life. I would like to share with you some of the things I have learned, but I also encourage you to be creative and then share your ideas with others. You can go to www.theloverevolution.com, which is the official website for the Love Revolution, and there you will find links to all the Love Revolution social network pages, graphics, downloads, and many tools you can use to help advance this movement. You can share your ideas with others as well as have the opportunity to learn from them. Remember...you are the Love Revolution! Without your active participation it won't work.

Here are some ideas we have collected from various people and found:

- When it is obvious that you and someone else want the same parking place, let the other person have it and do so with a smile on your face.
- Mow an elderly neighbor's lawn or shovel the snow in the winter.
- Clean an elderly person's house or offer to do the grocery shopping.
- Give someone without transportation a ride to church or another event, even if it is out of your way to do so.
- Truly listen to someone without interrupting.
- Be a polite driver.

- Hold a door open for a stranger and let him or her go ahead of you.
- If you have a cart filled with groceries and the person behind you has two items, let that person go first.
- Babysit for a single parent to give that person a bit of alone time or time to get a project done peacefully.
- Invite a person who has no family in town to your house for the holidays.
- Send cards and/or flowers to show appreciation.
- Give a single mom a gift certificate to take her children out to lunch.

It Works!

One of the ideas we received was: "Secretly pay for someone else's dinner in the restaurant where you are eating." Dave and I do this often and have had delightful results. We saw two elderly ladies in a restaurant one evening. They were all dressed up and looked as cute as could be. We felt a desire to pay for their dinner and did so through the waiter. We asked him to let us leave first and then tell them someone wanted to bless them with their meal. Of course, they asked who it was and the waiter shared that I was a minister on television and that we just wanted to put a smile on their faces.

Several months later, we were in the same restaurant and one of the ladies came over to us and asked if we remembered her. We must have seemed unsure, so she quickly repeated the incident, and then told us that night we bought her meal was her birthday and how much it meant to her that someone would do that. She said she went about searching for my television program and had been watching it ever since. We not only had the joy of making them happy but were extra blessed that God had used us on her birthday. She is also now receiving regular teaching from the Word of God through our television program and God only knows what the fruit of that will be. So one tiny act of kindness and a small financial investment not only brought joy, but introduced her to the Word of God.

Another suggestion we received was: "Pay for someone else's groceries at the grocery store." Our son shared a story that touched my heart and made me proud to be his mother. He and his wife were at the grocery store and he noticed a woman who looked tired, stressed, and as though she had very little money. She was shopping with her list and appeared to be using great caution as she put items into her basket. He simply walked up to her, gave her a one-hundred-dollar bill, told her to get the things she needed, and walked off. I read once that love waits in the shadows for an opportunity to express itself, steps out, and does its work, then quickly moves back in the shadows to wait for the next opportunity. I think that is a beautiful thought, don't you?

I frequently watch for people who seem to be discouraged and give them something monetary with the simple message, "God loves you." Many times, I don't even say anything about God, I simply show His character! I saw a young girl on her break at a Starbucks store where she worked. She was sitting alone at a table, looking very tired. I handed her fifty dollars and said, "I just want to bless you. I bet you work really hard and I want you to know I appreciate it." She looked shocked and then said, "That is the nicest thing anyone has ever done for me."

I don't think we realize how many people walk among us every day who feel lonely or insignificant and have had little or no experience with unconditional love. They are not accustomed to getting anything "free" or receiving anything they have not earned or deserved. I think doing random things for people just to be a blessing and for no other reason is an amazing way to show God's love.

Don't Forget to Do Good

Hebrews 13:16 urges us not to "forget or neglect to do kindness and good, to be generous and distribute and contribute to the needy [of the church, as embodiment and proof of fellowship], for such sacrifices are pleasing to God." Although this Scripture speaks specifically about doing these things for those in the church, the point I want to make is that living in this generous kind of way is pleasing to God. There are many other Scriptures that tell us to be good to everybody, not just those we consider to be like-minded with or who are in our church. For example, 1 Thessalonians 5:15 urges us to "always aim to show kindness and seek to do good to one another and to everybody."

Let me encourage you to think of things you can do for the people who serve you in ways such as picking up your trash or delivering the mail. These are people who are in our lives all the time, but we seldom think of what their jobs are like for them. I certainly would not want to smell and collect garbage all day.

My daughter once wrote a note of appreciation to her garbage collectors and gave them a gift card to get lunch. I think these things not only bless people, but can often be shocking too because they almost never happen. The world is filled with people who work hard doing jobs that are not very pleasant and yet nobody notices.

I once saw a woman cleaning the bathroom at a department store where I shop and I gave her some money and said, "You look like you work hard and I thought you could use a blessing." I smiled and quickly left. A few minutes later, she found me in the shoe department and expressed her gratitude and told me how this act of kindness lifted her up.

She told me that she did indeed work hard and felt nobody paid much attention to that fact. You'll be amazed at what will happen in your heart if you make a habit of noticing those who usually aren't noticed. God watches out for them and He will be delighted to have you make yourself available as His partner in this endeavor.

Practice Common Courtesy

When we solicited ideas for showing love to others, one person wrote: "Always say 'please' and 'thank you.'" These are two forms of common courtesy and certainly, being courteous instead of rude is a way to show kindness and respect for others. I want to especially encourage you to be courteous at home with your family. I am trying to remember to always say thank you to Dave when he has done something I have asked him to do. It is very important that we don't take our loved ones for granted. Having good manners in public should be an overflow of what we normally do at home behind closed doors.

Love is not rude, according to 1 Corinthians 13:5. Rudeness

usually results from selfishness, and one way to fight it is to use good manners at all times. Our society is filled with rudeness, harshness, and crudeness, but this does not display the character of God. Jesus said He is "not harsh, hard, sharp, or pressing" (Matt. 11:30), and we need to follow His example.

We certainly need to make a point of being thankful and expressing our gratitude. In several places the Bible makes the point that we are to, "Be thankful and say so." We may think we are thankful, grateful people, but what is in the heart does come out of our mouths (see Matt. 12:34). If we are indeed appreciative, expressing thanks should come naturally for us.

Time Is a Great Gift—Give Your Talent

Whatever your particular talent is, offer it as a gift occasionally rather than always wanting or expecting to be paid for it. For example, if you are a photographer offer to take wedding pictures free for a friend or someone on a tight budget.

If you are a hairdresser, offer to go to a homeless shelter and cut hair once a month or more if you're willing.

A friend of mine is a decorative painter and she recently spent three days painting free at a home for troubled young women.

God has given each of us abilities and we should use them to benefit one another.

I mentioned in chapter 3 a woman who had little money but wanted to support missions financially. She did so by selling her baked goods to raise money for missions. Her story emphasizes the point that if we will refuse to do nothing, we will be able to find the something that we can do, and when everyone gets involved it won't be long and the good in our world will overcome the evil.

Set Some Goals

Let's have goals! I am a strong believer in having goals and having a plan to reach them. You might suggest to your pastor that when everyone leaves church on Sunday they agree to do an act of random kindness within the next three hours. Just imagine what would happen if that got started worldwide!

In this chapter, I have highlighted just a few of the countless ways we can show love to others—ideas that hopefully help you understand the kind of things you can do. To say we cannot do anything is just not true. We may make excuses, but excuses are nothing more than a way to deceive ourselves and justify doing nothing. You will come alive as never before if you will aggressively reach out to others. Millions of people in the world feel they have no purpose, and they search for the will of God for their lives and live in confusion.

Let us not forget the words of Jesus: "I give you a new commandment: that you should love one another. Just as I have loved you, so you too should love one another" (John 13:34). Without a doubt, this is our purpose and the will of God for our lives.

CHAPTER
11

Find Out What People Need and Be Part of the Solution

I have become all things to all men.
1 Corinthians 9:22 NIV

Paul said that although he was free in every way from anyone's control, he had made himself a servant to everyone. That is a pretty amazing statement if you really think about it. He was free enough to give himself as a servant without the fear of being taken advantage of. He knew that in order to have real life, he had to give his life away. He decided to live to serve and make others happy. In his daily life, he was following the example Jesus had given him.

Paul went on to say that he became as a Jew to the Jews, as one under the law to those under the law, and to the weak he became weak (see 1 Cor. 9:22). In other words, he adjusted him-self to be whatever people needed him to be. He did whatever it took to win them to Christ and show love to them. Paul was highly educated, but I am sure that when he was with people who were not educated, he never spoke of his degrees or gave a discourse on everything he knew. He did not make a display of how educated he was. In fact, the following statement shows his humility and determination to never make others feel belittled. In fact, he wrote: "For I resolved to know nothing (to be acquainted with nothing, to make a display of the knowledge of nothing, and to be conscious of nothing) among you except Jesus Christ (the Messiah) and Him crucified" (1 Cor. 2:2).

When Paul was with people, he had to listen to them and take time to genuinely learn about them. I believe this is something we all need to do and I know from experience that doing so will enhance relationships in amazing ways. We should get to know people. We need to find out what they like and dislike, want or don't want, what they need, and what their dreams are for the future. If they are weak in an area and we are strong in that area, we should make sure we don't boast of our abilities.

Find Ways to Help People Feel Good about Themselves

I am fairly disciplined in my eating habits, and recently I spent a week with someone who really struggles in that area. The person mentioned several times how disciplined I am and how undisciplined she is. Each time she did so, I downplayed my ability to discipline myself by saying, "I have areas of weakness also, and you will overcome this as you continue to pray and make an effort."

There was a time in my life when I would not have been so sensitive to my friend's feelings. I would have probably given her a sermon about the benefits of discipline and the dangers of overeating and poor nutrition. However, I would not have succeeded in doing anything but making my friend feel guilty and condemned. When she asked me to share ideas that might help her I did so, but with an attitude that did not make her feel that I had it all together and she was a mess. I have discovered that one way to love people is to help them not to feel worse about the things they already feel bad about.

Meekness and humility are two of the most beautiful aspects of love. Paul said that love is not boastful and does not display itself haughtily (see 1 Cor. 13:4). Humility serves and always does what lifts others up.

The Bible teaches us to have the same attitude and humble mind that Jesus had (see Phil. 2:5). He was one with God, but stripped Himself of all privileges and humbled Himself to become like a human being so He could die in our place and take the punishment we deserved as sinners (see Phil. 2:6–9). He never made people feel badly because they were not on His level, but instead He stooped to their level. Paul did the same, and we need to follow these biblical examples.

We All Need Different Things

We are all different, and we each have different needs. I urge you to go the extra mile and find out what people really need instead of merely giving them what you want to give them. Perhaps you can easily give people words of encouragement, so you tend to encourage everyone. This is good because everyone needs some words of encouragement, but you might be giving those words to people who really need you to see that they need practical help in some way. They may be three months behind on their rent and instead of you encouraging them that God will provide, they actually need you to help them pay the rent. If you are not able to help financially that is understandable, but it is always good to at least consider doing something tangible to go along with words when the situation is serious.

Perhaps you love to spend time with people. You like to visit, call people and talk on the phone, or have friends to your home for meals—so you often try to give your time in these ways. But what if you are giving time to people who actually need more time to be alone and relax. They would be blessed if you gave them a gift certificate to go to lunch while you watched their children, but you keep trying to give them what you enjoy.

Some people are very detailed. They think and talk in great detail. They may send very long e-mails or leave voice messages that seem to be endless. Some people dread even beginning reading e-mails or listening to messages from these highly detailed people because they know doing so will take a long time. If those who are detail oriented only do what pleases them or what they like, they will find some people avoiding them.

Even in communication, we should find out what people want and need and not simply speak and write in ways that please us. If you have a friend who likes details, then give that person all you can think of. If, on the other hand, your friends prefer the bottom line, then give them "just the facts."

I like to give gifts, so I usually do that to show love. I once had an assistant who did not seem to appreciate my gifts very much. This really bothered me because she seemed ungrateful, but when I got to know her better she told me that the most important thing to her was hearing words that conveyed love. I wanted to give her gifts because that was easier for me than saying the words she wanted to hear. I show appreciation for someone's hard work by giving them things, but she needed me to *tell* her frequently what a good job she was doing and how much I appreciated her. She needed hugs or pats on the back. Through gift-giving, I was trying really hard to show her love, but amazingly she did not feel loved. I think that happens more often than we realize simply because we don't learn enough about people to be able to give them what they truly need, we simply want to give them what we want to give them because that is easier for us.

When we expect everyone to be alike, we end up pressuring them to be something they don't know how to be. God graciously provides for every need we have. He places the right people in our lives with the right gifts if we can only see it and appreciate people for who they are.

Study People

Studying people to educate myself concerning what they need from me was an eye-opening experience. For example, my husband needs respect and to know that I feel he is doing a good job taking care of me. He needs a peaceful atmosphere to live in. He loves sports of all kinds and needs time to play golf and watch ballgames. If I give him those things, he is as happy as he can be.

I, on the other hand, love acts of service. It means a lot to me when someone does something for me that will make my life easier. My husband almost always cleans the kitchen after dinner so I can sit and rest. If he sees me trying to do something that seems hard for me, such as carrying a heavy object, he immediately tells me to put it down and let him do it for me. These things make me feel valuable and loved. Understanding what each other needs and being willing to give it has improved our relationship tremendously.

My daughter Sandra needs quality time and words of encouragement. My daughter Laura needs words of encouragement, but spending time with me is not as important to her. Both of my daughters love me very much, but they show it in different ways. Sandra calls me almost every day, and she and her family eat with us often. Laura doesn't call as frequently and I don't see her as much as I do Sandra, but she helps me take care of my elderly mother and aunt by getting their groceries and helping with banking issues and paying bills, even though she has four children at home and her husband's grandmother lives with them.

I have two sons who are both wonderful, but they are very different. One calls me every day and tells me he loves me; the other one does not call as much, but shows his love in other ways. Anytime I ask either of them to do something for me, they either do it or get it done. My point is that our children are all different, but all wonderful.

I have also had to study my children and learn what each of them needs from me so I can give it to them. One likes receiving gifts, another likes time, another needs words of encouragement, while another may need a display of affection. I am still learning all the time, but at least now I am trying to please *them* instead of myself.

We all have a "love language," a term popularized by Dr. Gary Chapman and explained in his book *The Five Love Languages*. A person's love language is the way he or she expresses and receives love. As I mentioned, my love language is acts of service, while my daughter's is quality time. When people speak to us in our specific love language, we feel loved, and when we speak someone else's love language, they feel loved. We usually try to give people what we need—to speak to them in our love language, but that can be a huge mistake. If they don't need what we need, then no matter how hard we work at it, they will still feel unloved.

I am also learning that no matter how much I need something, the person I want it from may not be equipped to give it to me, at least not at the present time. I spent a lot of years discouraged and disappointed until I finally learned to pray and trust God to give me what I needed through the people He chose. In the meantime, I try to do what is right and I find that my joy increases not because I get everything I want, but by giving others what they want. I don't always (or even usually) enjoy the sacrifice part, but I do like the inner satisfaction from knowing I am doing what God wants me to do.

Have you studied the people in your life to find out what they need from you and then been willing to give it to them? Have you ever asked them what they need? It is time for us to stop living selfishly and merely doing what is comfortable for us. We need to get to know the people that God has placed in our lives and set about the business of serving them for their good rather than ours.

Meet the Needs of Others

The Bible teaches that if we are strong in faith we ought to bear with the failings of the weak and not live to please ourselves. Each one of us should make it a practice to please and make our neighbors happy for their good, to edify, strengthen, and build them up (see Rom. 15:1–2). This is wonderful advice, but we usually do the opposite. We want others to live to make *us* happy and do what pleases *us*. The result is that no matter what people do, we are never happy and satisfied.

Man's ways do not work. They don't provide what we truly want and need, but God's ways do work. If we do as He instructs we may make some sacrifices, but we will have a kind of joy that cannot be found anywhere except in the center of God's will.

Will you be honest and ask yourself some questions that may be difficult to answer but will bring you face-to-face with where you are in the whole theme of loving other people?

- How much do you do for others?
- Are you trying to find out what people want and need so you can help?
- Are you sincerely trying to know the people in your life in a genuine way?
- How much do you really even know the people in your own family?

As I answered these questions a few years ago, I was appalled at the level of selfishness in my life even though I had been a Christian minister for many years. The truth began to open my eyes about why I was still unhappy and unfulfilled even though I had every reason to be really happy. The bottom line was that I was selfish and self-centered and I needed to change. These changes did not come easily or quickly, neither are they completed, but as I press on daily I am making progress and I am happier all the time.

Learn to Listen

Once I made up my mind that I was declaring war on selfishness and wanted to be part of a Love Revolution, I needed to find creative ways to be a blessing. Since people are different and need different things, I had to start training myself to really listen to what they told me. I find that if I listen to anyone for very long I can walk away with the knowledge of something I can get them, do for them, or pray about for them if I really want to. The "I don't know what to do" excuse is an old one and needs to be put in the trash. If we really want to give we can find ways to do it. Remember, "Indifference makes excuses, but love finds a way!"

"Indifference makes excuses, but love finds a way!"

I believe this matter of listening is a huge part of learning to love people the way they need to be loved. Take a week and during that time write down what people tell you in general conversation that they want, need, or like. Pray over the list and ask God if He would have you do any of it or, if you have a desire to do any of it, then go for it. I don't believe you need a special word from God to begin blessing people. If what they need is too much for you to do on your own, then I suggest you consider getting a few other people to join with you and meet the need as a group. If a friend mentions that she is still sleeping on the couch after being in her apartment for a year because she has not been able to afford a bedroom set, getting her one would be a good thing to consider as a group project.

A friend was talking to me about a young man at her church who had terribly crooked teeth. They were so bad that he refused to smile because he was embarrassed for anyone to see them. I was moved with compassion when I heard his story and we were able to anonymously provide for his teeth to be fixed. That changed his life. How often do we hear of something like that, feel compassion and yet walk away without even considering whether or not we could do something to help? I think it is far too often. We simply need to be educated and retrained. We need to form new habits. Instead of assuming that there is nothing we can do, we should at least think about it. Remember, 1 John 3:17 says: "If anyone has this world's goods (resources for sustaining life) and sees his brother and fellow believer in need, yet closes his heart of compassion against him, how can the love of God live and remain in him?"

I heard a friend say she needed skin care products. I had an extra set, so I gave her one. My mom mentioned she was out of perfume, so I got her a bottle. My aunt likes to go to Starbucks, so I got her a gift card. Please understand that I am not sharing these things with you for any reason other than to give you ideas about ways you can show love to the people in your world. I'm sure you have plenty of ideas of your own, so please remember to go to the Love Revolution website and share them so you can inspire us.

Each time we act to improve the life of another person or strike out against injustice, we send forth a ripple of hope in what appears to be a hopeless society. We really can overcome evil with good, so let's be relentless in our determination to do so.

CHAPTER
12

Unconditional Love

Love is not blind—it sees more, not less.
Rabbi Julius Gordon

One of the most beautiful things the Bible says is that while we were still sinners, Christ died for us (see Rom. 5:8). He did not wait for us to deserve His love; He loves us unconditionally. To be honest, that's hard for many of us to comprehend because we are so accustomed to having to earn and deserve everything in life.

God is rich in mercy, and in order to satisfy the great, wonderful, and intense love with which He loves us, He poured His life out for us freely (see Eph. 2:4). *That* is revolutionary love! Real, revolutionary love must give itself, for it can never be satisfied to do anything less.

It is God's unconditional love that draws us to Him, and it is our unconditional love toward others in His name that will draw others to Him. He wants us to love people in His place and do it the same way He would if He were here in bodily form. *He wants us to live the Love Revolution.*

You may remember the story I told in chapter 6 about my father and how God instructed Dave and me to take care of him even though he certainly did not deserve it. Showing him the unconditional love of God eventually softened his hard heart, and he repented of his sin and received Jesus as his Savior.

Human love finds it impossible to love unconditionally, but we have the love of God in us as believers in Jesus Christ, and we can let that love flow freely, without conditions. Man's love fails, but God's does not. Man's love comes to an end, but God's does not. Sometimes I find that although I cannot love a person in my own human strength, I am able to love them with God's love.

Someone who hurt me repeatedly for years recently asked me how I felt about them. Did I love them? I was honestly able to say that although I did not have the fond feelings for them I could have had if things had been different, I did love them as a child of God and would help them in their need.

The true love of God doesn't depend on feelings; it is based on decision. I will help anyone who needs help, unless helping them would ultimately hurt them. They don't have to deserve it. As a matter of fact, sometimes I think the less they deserve it, the more beautiful and impacting it is. It is absolutely freeing to be able to love people without stopping to ask if they deserve it.

Forgiveness

It was out of the question...simply too much too ask. How could Bill Ebarb forgive the man who killed his brother in cold blood? Bill Ebarb and Charles Manuel were two strangers whose lives would be forever intertwined in a split second—the moment Charles pulled the trigger and murdered Bill's brother, John. From that moment on, Bill could think of nothing but revenge.

Bill's heart was full of rage and anger, and he was convinced that no punishment had the ability to wipe away his loss. After John was killed, there wasn't a day that went by that Bill didn't think about the killer. The intense hatred was eating him alive. This obsession soon cost Bill his job and his marriage. He knew that if he continued down this destructive path, it would soon cost him his life.

That's when Bill experienced a change in his life that was even more powerful than the day he lost his brother. Bill experienced the forgiveness of Christ. This was something supernatural and beyond any forgiveness that a human could manage alone. God removed the hatred—He removed the anger.

Bill's heart was so miraculously transformed that he began to think the impossible. He realized that if the Lord could forgive him for all of the things that he had done in his life, he must also forgive Charles. And he must tell Charles that he had forgiven him for murdering his brother. At first it was an act of obedience, but then it became a matter of the heart. And so eighteen years to the day of John's death, Bill and Charles sat across from each other in a meeting that confirmed what God had already done in both of their lives. God had set both of these men free through the power of forgiveness.

Statistics[1] say:

- Forgiveness reduces stress. Nursing a grudge can place the same strains—tense muscles, elevated blood pressure, increased sweating—on your body as a major stressful event.
- Your heart will benefit if you're able to forgive. A study found a link between forgiving and improvements in heart rate and blood pressure.
- A recent study found that women who were able to forgive their spouses and feel kindhearted toward them resolved conflicts more effectively.

Human love depends on feelings. We love people because they have been good to us, they helped us, or they loved us first. They make us feel good about ourselves, or they make our life easier, so we say we love them. Or we love them because we want them to love us. But that type of love is based on what they are doing, and if they stop doing it we will probably stop loving them. That kind of love comes and goes; it is hot and then cold. That is the kind of love we experience in the world. Many marriages and other personal relationships are based on that kind of love. We love ice cream because it tastes good, and we love people because they give us nice Christmas gifts.

God's love is totally different—it is not based on anything except God Himself. And when we receive Christ as our Savior, the love of God is poured into our hearts by the Holy Spirit (see Rom. 5:5). When we become partners with God, He expects us to be His representatives in the earth and He equips us with the love we need to do the job He asks us to do. When human love ends, which it often does, God's love is still available to finish what needs to be done.

I did not love my father as a girl might because he was never a father to me. But I did have the love of God in me, and I was able to decide totally apart from feelings that I would treat him kindly in his old age and be merciful toward him. I actually felt compassion for him because he wasted his entire life and had memories full of regrets.

We often hear amazing stories of forgiveness. I heard of a teenager who was drinking and caused an accident that killed a man's wife and child. The man knew God wanted him to forgive the young man who caused the accident, and through much prayer he was able to let the love of God flow through him. That man was a love revolutionary!

We must learn to look at what people have done to themselves rather than what they have done to us. Usually, when someone hurts another, he or she has probably damaged him- or herself at least as much and is probably suffering some fallout as a result. That is precisely what Jesus did when He said, "Father, forgive them, for they know not what they do" (Luke 23:34).

The God kind of love cannot be grasped with the mind; it is a matter of the heart. It seemed quite unreasonable for God to ask me to take care of my father—but then, love is quite unreasonable, isn't it? There is no reason for God to love us while we are sinning and totally ignoring Him, but He does.

Mercy Triumphs over Judgment

It is easy to judge a person or situation and dole out only what is deserved, but mercy is greater than that. It is a glorious thing for someone to overlook an offense. In order to help people in third-world countries, I cannot look at the fact that many of them worship idols or animals or the sun or even demons. I could easily say, "No wonder they're starving—they have turned their backs on God." But perhaps I would be in the same situation they're in if I had been born where they were. We must remind ourselves, "If it were not for the grace of God in my life, that could be me."

It is easy for some religious people to look at a homosexual man who has AIDS and think, *He deserves it*. But is that the way God looks at the man? Or does God see the real "why" behind the "what"? God wants to reach out to that man with redemption as long as the man draws breath—and He may want to use me or you to do it. That does not mean we need to embrace others' sin, but we should embrace *people* and help them in their time of need, by providing medicine, shelter, and kind words that enable them to find hope in God.

Mercy and compassion are two of the most beautiful qualities of love, and in fact there is no real love without them. Because I was forced to earn everything I got during my first thirty years of life, I wasn't big on giving people what I had worked for when it seemed to me that they had done nothing to help themselves. Learning the difference between my human love and the love of God that had been deposited in me took some time. Mercy cannot be earned or deserved. Paul wrote to the Colossians and told them to "put on love" (see Col. 3:14). I love the phrase "put on," which means to do something on purpose, without depending on feelings or reason. I have learned amazing life lessons from that tiny little phrase.

As I write this, it is the middle of the afternoon, and I am still sitting in my pajamas writing. Dave just called and wants to come and pick me up and go to a Mustang car show. I can assure you that going to the car show will be an act of love. I don't feel like getting dressed and ready; I am rather enjoying the whole pajama thing—but I will do it. In the same way, we all encounter numerous opportunities to choose to put on unconditional love.

Unless we learn to live beyond our feelings, we will never be able to love people with the love of God or help the needy people of the world. Are you ready to put on mercy? Are you ready to put on love? If you are struggling with feelings that could prevent you from doing the right thing, ask yourself, "What would Jesus do in this situation?" I know for sure that if Dave had given up on me, I would not be the person I am today. He listened to his heart, not his emotions, and that is what I am encouraging you to do.

Love Doesn't Just Walk Away

Loving people does not mean letting them take advantage of us. It does not mean giving them a free ride in life while they do nothing. The Bible says that God corrects and disciplines everyone He loves (see Heb. 12:6). Correction is not punishment; it is training in right behavior. Sometimes that training requires the withholding of blessings, but God will always meet our basic needs when we cry out to Him. The Bible says that we can encounter trials of all kinds and if we need wisdom we can ask of the giving God who gives to all liberally and He will help us without reproach or faultfinding (see James 1:1–5). That is a beautiful thought!

I may not buy a drug addict a new car since I know he may likely sell it to buy drugs, but I can feed him and give him a place to take a shower and give him hope of a new life. I can tell him God loves him and wants to help him, and I can refrain from judging him, for if I judge him I won't be able to love him.

Often when people hurt us or are difficult to get along with, we just want to get them out of our lives, but what if God wants us instead to build a relationship with them? It is much easier on us to merely walk away or shut difficult people out of our lives, but that is not always what God wants. We must learn what love really looks like in every situation and apply it without giving in to feelings or the lack of them.

One of the questions I am asked frequently is, "How long should I stick with this person?" That is a question that only your heart can answer. God is the only one who understands the entire situation from both sides, and He will guide you in your decisions if you truly want to do His will rather than your own. Just remember: Joining the Love Revolution means being ready and willing to love others even when it seems impossible.

When I discuss unconditional love with people, another question that always comes up is, "Am I just supposed to keep giving no matter what people do?" The answer to that question is no.

Suppose a family member has had a drug and alcohol problem for most of his or her adult life, and in addition is very irresponsible. The family spends tremendous time, money, and effort to help him, but eventually he always goes back to his old habits and lifestyle. This is the sort of situation where the enemy uses this family member's weakness to distract and steal strength from those who love him and have tried to help. Sometimes we have to face the fact that no matter how much we want to help someone, it never works unless they really want to be helped. In fact, very often, after years of continually trying to help, usually at great personal sacrifice, the family has to refuse to help any longer. This is not a decision that can be made quickly or easily, but often it has to be made.

Sometimes as Christians, we are accused of not truly practicing the love of Christ when a situation like this arises. We hear things like, "How can you claim to love people when you won't even help your own relatives?" Though it's difficult, the loving thing to do is to be firm and say, "If you ever really want to face your issues and get real help, let us know," but I also know that I cannot keep on enabling him or her to continue a destructive lifestyle.

We should not let a loved one in trouble be hungry or sick with no help, but we also must not allow him to steal our peace or merely use us. Loving people does not mean doing for them what they should be doing for themselves.

Mercy helps those who don't deserve help, but unconditional love is not intended to allow people to be irresponsible while we pay the bill. Mercy gives many opportunities, and unconditional love never gives up. It prays and is ready to move out of the shadows and help when doing so will really make a difference.

God wants His love to flow through us and into others. We need to learn to love ourselves in a balanced way, for we must love ourselves or we will have no love to give away. We need to receive God's love and let it heal us. Remember that we cannot give away what we don't have. But we must not stop there! God heals us so we can bring healing to others. God wants us to transition from those who have been rescued to those who are rescuing others. Human love always comes to an end, but thankfully the love of God does not. God promises us that His love never fails!

CHAPTER
13

Love Keeps No Record of Wrong

Love does not delight in evil but rejoices with
the truth. It always protects, always trusts,
always hopes, always perseveres.
1 Corinthians 13:6–7 NIV

Are you a good accountant? Do you keep precise, detailed records of the wrongs that have been done to you? For many years, each time Dave and I had an argument, I would dig into my mental files and start bringing up all the other things he had done that I felt were wrong. I reminded him of past mistakes, and he was amazed that I even remembered many of them because they were so old. I recall one time when he said, "Where do you keep all this stuff stored?" While I held on to things for years, Dave was quick to forgive and let go.

More than anything God wants us to love one another, but that is impossible without total forgiveness. We cannot genuinely love those we are angry at or resentful toward. Paul wrote to the Corinthians and said, "Love (God's love in us) does not insist on its own rights or its own way, for it is not self-seeking; it is not touchy or fretful or resentful; it takes no account of the evil done to it [it pays no attention to a suffered wrong]" (1 Corinthians 13:5b).

Believe the Best

If we want to love people, we must let God transform the way we think about people and the things they do. We can believe the worst and be suspicious of everything others do and say, but real love always believes the best. What we think and believe is a choice. The root of much of our trouble in life is that we don't control or discipline our thoughts. By not choosing to discipline our thoughts, we automatically do choose to believe the worst of someone or be suspicious.

The prophet Jeremiah asked the people this, "How long will you allow these grossly offensive thoughts to lodge within you?" (see Jer. 4:14). The thoughts they chose to think were offensive to God.

When we choose to believe the best, we are able to let go of everything which could be harmful to good relationships. I've saved a lot of energy that would have been used up by anger simply by saying to myself, "Even though what they said or did hurt me, I choose to believe their heart was right." I keep talking to myself until my feelings of anger start to dissipate. I say things like, "I don't believe they really understood how their actions affected me. I don't believe they would try to hurt me on purpose. They just don't understand how it sounds when they say that. Maybe they don't feel good physically today or perhaps they are having a personal problem that is making them insensitive to how they are behaving."

I know from experience that keeping mental records of offenses poisons our own lives and does not really change the other person. Many times we waste a day being angry at someone who doesn't even realize they did anything that bothered us. They are enjoying their day and we are wasting ours.

If we are going to keep records, then why not keep records of the good things people say and do rather than the mistakes they make?

Examples of negative record keeping:

Dave watches sports all the time, and he knows I don't enjoy them.

Dave corrects me on details when I am trying to tell a story.

When I need understanding, Dave tries to give me advice.

In forty-two years of marriage I can count on one hand how many times Dave has sent me flowers.

Dave planned a golf outing with his friends and did not even ask me what I was going to do or if I had any plans.

Examples of positive record keeping:

Dave is always willing to quickly forgive me when I behave wrongly toward him.

Dave gives me total freedom to be myself.

Dave picks up after himself. He is not a person who leaves messes for other people to clean up.

Dave tells me every day that he loves me, and quite often several times a day.

Dave compliments me about my clothes and appearance.

Dave buys me anything I want that we can afford.

Dave is always willing to take me anywhere I want to go.

Dave is very stable in his moods. He is rarely ever grouchy.

Dave is very protective of me. I feel safe when I am with him.

It is easy to see that the positive list is longer than the negative one, and I imagine it would be that way with most people if they would take time to write down the good things. We should look for and celebrate the good in the world and in people because we overcome evil with good. Thinking and talking about the good in people will cause us to barely notice the things that once really bothered us.

Don't Grieve the Holy Spirit

We can actually cause the Holy Spirit to feel sad through our anger, bad temper, unforgiveness, bitterness, quarreling, and contention. The Bible urges us to banish ill will, spite, and baseness of any kind. It makes me sad to think that I could make the Holy Spirit of God sad. When I remember how easily angered I once was, I know I did grieve Him, and I don't want to do it ever again. The only way I can avoid it is to be aggressive about letting go of ill feelings toward others as soon as they arise. We are to be useful, helpful, and kind to one another, forgiving one another readily and freely as God in Christ forgave us (see Eph. 4:30–32).

Our anger makes the Holy Spirit sad not only because God wants us to love one another but because He knows how negatively it affects us, and He wants us to enjoy a life of freedom. We should be imitators of God and follow His example. He is slow to anger, has plenty of mercy, and is quick to forgive. Our anger does not promote the righteousness God calls us to live in.

Just as genuine love has nothing to do with how we feel, genuine forgiveness doesn't either. Both are based on a decision we make, not a feeling we have. I have learned that if I choose to forgive, my feelings eventually catch up with my decision. Forgiving others enables me to talk to them rather than shut them out of my life. It allows me to pray for them and to speak blessing to and about them rather than negative, evil things. We pay too much attention to our feelings. Instead, we should remember that our feelings are fickle and quite changeable. What does not change is love.

Make Allowances for One Another

If we truly love one another, we will bear with one another and make allowances for one another (see Eph. 4:1–2). Making allowances doesn't mean making excuses for people's wrong behavior—if it is wrong then it is wrong, and pretending or ignoring it does not help. But making allowances for one another means we allow each other to be less than perfect. We send messages with our words and attitude that say, "I won't reject you because you did that; I won't give up on you. I will work through this with you and believe in you."

I have told my children that even though I might not always agree with everything they do, I will always try to understand and will never stop loving them. I want them to know that they can count on me to be a constant in their life.

God knows all about our faults and He still chooses us. He knows the mistakes we will make before we make them, and His posture toward us is, "I will allow you to be imperfect!" He promises to never leave us or forsake us (see Heb. 13:5).

Dave allows me to be me even though everything about me is less than perfect. He never pressures me to "change or else!" I never fear being rejected by him for being an imperfect wife. There are things about each person in our family and other close relationships that we wish were different, but when we really love someone we accept all of them. We accept the good and the not so good. The truth is that there just are no perfect people. If we expect perfection, we always set ourselves up for disappointment and even bitterness. Making allowances for one another makes life a lot easier, and even more important it demonstrates our obedience to God.

When people do something that you just don't understand, instead of trying to figure them out, tell yourself, "They are human." Jesus knew the nature of human beings and therefore He was not shocked when they did things He wished they would not have done. He still loved Peter even though Peter denied even knowing Him. He still loved His disciples even though they were unable to stay awake and pray with Him in His hour of agony and suffering. What people do will not stop us from loving them if we realize ahead of time they are not going to be perfect and prepare to make allowance for that human tendency that we all have.

Not only should we not keep records of what others do wrong, but we should not keep records of what we believe we do right. Thinking too highly of ourselves is what causes us to be impatient and unmerciful toward other people. The apostle Matthew said that when we do a good deed we should not let our right hand know what our left hand did (see Matt. 6:3). To me this means I shouldn't meditate on what I believe my good deeds were or what my good traits are. I just need to concentrate on showing love to everyone I meet. That's the primary focus of a Love Revolutionary!

Love Covers Sin

The apostle Peter said that above all things we should have intense and unfailing love for one another, for love covers a multitude of sins (see 1 Peter 4:8). Love doesn't just cover one mistake; it covers a multitude. God's love for us not only covered our sins, it actually paid the price to completely remove them. Love is a powerful cleansing agent. I want you to notice that Peter said to do this—love—above all other things.

Paul had the same message for the Colossians, urging them to put on love above all (see Col. 3:14). Over and over in the Bible we see the constant reminder to love one another and not let anything stand in the way of doing so.

When Peter asked Jesus how many times he would be expected to forgive a brother for the same offense, Jesus told him to keep on doing it as many times as it took (see Matt. 18:21–22). Peter suggested seven times, and I have often wondered if he was already at six and thought he had only one more effort in him. If we are going to join the Love Revolution, we must understand that a lot of forgiveness will be required. In fact, it will probably be part of our daily experience. Some of the things we need to forgive may be minor and fairly easy, but occasionally that big thing comes along and we start wondering if we can ever get over it. Just remember that God never tells us to do anything unless He gives us the ability to do it. We can forgive anyone for anything if we let the God kind of love flow through us.

When we cover people's faults we are blessed, and when we uncover them we are cursed. Part of covering someone's failure is keeping it private. Don't be quick to tell others what you know about someone else's faults. Keep people's secrets just as you would like them to keep yours. We see an account in the Bible of a time when Noah got drunk and lay naked in his tent. One of his sons exposed his nakedness by telling the other two brothers about it, and he received a curse on his life from that day forward. The two sons who were told walked backward into the tent so they would not see their father's nakedness, and they covered him. The Bible tells us that they were blessed (see Gen. 9:20–27). Noah's nakedness refers to his error in judgment, his mistake, his sin. As this story demonstrates so clearly, we are to cover one another, not expose one another's faults.

Jesus gave instructions about how to handle it when a brother wrongs you (see Matt. 18:15–17). He said the first thing to do is to go to him privately and talk to him about it. If that doesn't work, take two or three others with you in the hopes that he will come to his senses and repent. If we would follow these simple instructions, a great deal of trouble would be avoided. I can't tell you how many times people come to me to solve things they should be dealing with privately—things that should be between them and the person they feel has wronged them. Don't be fearful of confronting someone if you really feel you need to. Sometimes the quickest way to forgive is to get the issue out in the open and discuss it. Hidden offenses are like untreated infections. They silently get worse until they have infected an entire area and we are sick. We need to clean the wound immediately, before it is too late.

The Bible tells the story of a man named Joseph who was sold into slavery by his brothers. When Joseph's brothers discovered years later that he was alive and in charge of the food supply they desperately needed, they were afraid. They remembered how badly they had treated Joseph and so did he, but he chose not to reveal it to anyone else. He spoke with them privately and simply told them he was not God and vengeance belonged to God, not to him. He freely forgave them, urged them not to be afraid, and proceeded to provide for them and their families. No wonder Joseph was a powerful leader who found favor everywhere he went. He knew the power of love and the importance of total forgiveness!

Clear All Your Records

Why not get out all the past-due accounts you have kept on anyone and mark them, "Paid in full"? "Blessed is the man whose sin the Lord will never count against him" (Rom. 4:8 NIV). That does not mean that God does not see the sin. It means that because of love He does not charge it against the sinner. Love can acknowledge that a wrong has been done and erase it before it becomes lodged in the heart. Love does not register or record the wrong; this way resentment does not have a chance to grow.

Some of us worry about our memory, but to be truthful we probably need to get better at forgetting some things. I think we often forget what we should remember and remember what we should forget. Perhaps one of the most godlike things we can ever do in life is to forgive and forget. Some people say, "I will forgive them, but I will never forget it." The reality of that statement is that if we cling to the memory, we are not truly forgiving. You might ask how we can forget things that have hurt us. The answer is that we must *choose* not to think about it. When those things come to mind, we must cast down the thoughts and choose to think about things that will benefit us.

Clearing all your records will produce good results. It will relieve pressure and improve the quality of your life. Intimacy between you and God will be restored, and your joy and peace will increase. Your health may even improve because a calm and undisturbed mind and heart are the life and health of the body (see Prov. 14:30). Resentment builds walls. Love builds bridges!

CHAPTER
14

Practical Ways to Show Love

Preach the gospel at all times and when
necessary use words.
St. Francis of Assisi

This book is useless if I don't offer practical ways you can begin immediately showing love. As I have said previously, love is not a theory or mere talk, it is action. As Love Revolutionaries, we should constantly be looking for new and better ways to bring love into this world.

Let me remind you that no matter what we have or do, if we have not love then we have nothing and we are nothing (see 1 Cor. 13:1–3). It is imperative to the future of society that we begin aggressively showing love. People today are desperate to know whether God exists or not, what their purpose is for being here, and why the world is so filled with evil if God does indeed exist. I believe if they can see love in action, that will answer their questions. God is love and He does exist, and one

> No matter what we have or do, if we have not love then we have nothing and we are nothing.

major way He reveals Himself is through His people. The world needs to see the qualities of love lived out. They need to see patience, kindness, unselfishness, and willingness to forgive. They need to see people sacrificing to help others who are less fortunate. Being touched by love is like snuggling up in front of a fire under a warm, fuzzy blanket. It's a feeling like nothing else. And we have the power to give that gift to others!

Be Patient

The first quality of love listed in Paul's discourse in 1 Corinthians 13 in the Bible is patience. Paul writes that love endures long and is patient. Love is long-suffering. It remains steady and consistent when things are not going the way you wish they would.

I have been practicing being patient with clerks who are slow, who can't find prices for items, who run out of register tape, or who linger on the phone trying to calm down an irate customer when I am standing right there, waiting to be helped. I have had several store clerks actually thank me for being patient. I am sure they take a lot of abuse from frustrated, impatient, unloving customers, and I have decided I don't want to add to the problem; I want to be part of the answer. Sure, we are all in a hurry and want to get waited on right away, but since love is not self-seeking we must learn to put how the clerk feels ahead of how we feel. Recently a store clerk apologized for being so slow and I told her that nothing I was doing was so important that I could not wait. I saw her visibly relax and I realized that I had just shown her love.

We are encouraged in the Bible to be very patient with everybody, always keeping our temper in check (see 1 Thess. 5:14). That is not only good for our witness to other people, but it's also good for us. The more patient we are, the less stress we have! Peter said that the Lord is extraordinarily patient with us because it is His desire that none of us perish (see 2 Pet. 3:9). That is the same reason we should be patient with one another and especially with those in the world who are looking for God.

Paul told Timothy that servants of the Lord must be skilled and suitable teachers, mild-tempered, willing to suffer wrong, kind and patient with everyone (see 2 Tim. 2:24). We teach people every day by our actions. Teaching is done not only with words—action is often even more effective. We all have influence, and we should be careful how we use it. It doesn't do me or Christ's reputation any good to wear my rhinestone Jesus pendant and then be impatient and unloving with a sales clerk. To be honest, I've seen enough of that kind of stuff in the past twenty years to make me sick to my stomach.

We should not wear symbols of our Christian faith if we are not prepared to live up to it. The proof of my relationship with God is not my bumper sticker or my Christian jewelry or my record of church attendance. It is not how many Scriptures I have memorized or how extensive my Christian library is of books, DVDs, and CDs. The proof of my Christianity is seen in the fruit of Revolutionary Love.

I urge you to pray regularly that you will be able to endure whatever comes with a good temper. Trust me, things will come that have the ability to upset you, but if you are prepared ahead of time, you will be able to remain calm as you face those things. Displaying stability in our moods and temperament is very important. Too many people in the world are explosive when things don't go their way. I sincerely believe that one of the ways we can make an impact is to be patient when things go wrong.

A few weeks ago I preached on patience and being thankful no matter what your circumstances. I had done three major conferences in six weeks in addition to fulfilling several other commitments, and that Saturday morning session was the last of that string of commitments. I was really looking forward to getting home early that day, eating a good meal, having Dave take me shopping for a while, taking a hot bath at home, eating ice cream, and watching a good movie. You can see I was prepared to reward myself for my hard work. I had a good plan for myself!

We got on the plane to return home, and the flight was scheduled to be only thirty-five minutes. I was so thrilled . . . and then something went wrong. The airplane door wouldn't shut properly so we sat for almost an hour and a half while they worked on the door. There was talk of not being able to fly out that day and perhaps renting cars and driving home. I cannot tell you how hard it was for me to be patient. Just keeping my mouth shut was a huge accomplishment. I had preached on patience but forgotten to pray that if I was tested I would pass the test with flying colors.

Have you ever had the experience of hearing a great sermon that you really needed and finding yourself being tested on it in life immediately? Well, you should try preaching and see how quickly you're tested then! I realize we may not always feel patient, but we can still discipline ourselves to be patient. I can't do anything about how I feel sometimes, but I can control how I behave and so can you. I can assure you that I did not feel patient sitting on that runway, but I kept praying, *Oh God, please help me stay calm so I am not a poor witness for what I just finished preaching.* God helped me, and while things don't always turn out the way I want them to in those situations, in that case we ended up getting home in plenty of time for me to still do all the things I had planned.

When you find yourself in difficult situations, make an effort to hold your peace and you will see God work in your behalf. When the Israelites were between the Red Sea and the Egyptian army, Moses said, "The Lord will fight for you, and you shall hold your peace and remain at rest" (Exod. 14:14).

Give Time

Time is the most valuable commodity most of us have. When we ask people to give us their time, we should realize that we are asking for a valuable gift and we should greatly appreciate it when we get it. People frequently ask for my time, and unfortunately I cannot give it to all of them. If I tried, not only would I burn out but I would not have time to finish what God has given me to do during my life on earth.

We cannot say yes to everyone, but we should not say no to everyone either. I highly recommend giving some time away because it is a way to demonstrate love. I recently spoke at a church in Tennessee as a favor to a friend, and while I was there I sensed the Lord nudging me to return the offering they received for me that night to help the poor in their city. I realized right away that God wanted me to give my time and money freely. He wanted me to get nothing out of it except the joy of giving, which was more than enough. I find that God tests me in this way a couple of times each year and I am glad He does because I don't ever want to get into the habit of thinking I need to get something out of everything I do for others.

I confess that it is harder for me to give my time than it is to give my money or other possessions. At this point, I have lived at least two-thirds of my life, and I realize that what I have left needs to be focused and purposeful. Out of necessity I find myself needing to say no more often, yet I do say yes when I can since I know that my time is a valuable gift of love.

When someone helps you move, they are giving you the valuable gift of time. When you get someone's undivided attention, they are honoring you and showing love. Each time we ask, "Can you do something for me?" we are asking for the most valuable thing a person has because we are asking for a block of their time.

Think about your time. Be sure to give plenty of it to developing an intimate relationship with God, and make sure you give some of it to His people as a demonstration of His love. Tommy Barnett, senior pastor of Phoenix First Assembly of God, one of the fastest growing churches in America, said, "Life is something we are constantly losing." That is why we should take everything we do seriously. When people say they have nothing to give, they are forgetting that as long as we are alive we have something to give: our time.

Since time is such a valuable commodity, we should give it away purposefully and wisely. Don't let people steal your time, don't waste your time, and never say, "I'm just trying to kill a little time." Know what your priorities are and devote your time to those things. God and family should be at the top of your list. You also need to give time to taking care of yourself. You need to work, to rest, and to play in order to be a balanced individual. You also need to give some of your time away helping people who need you.

If you think you don't have time to get everything done and still give to others, I encourage you to do what God told Tommy Barnett to do. He told him to use his half hours wisely. He showed him that he had several half-hour spaces. Pastor Barnett says that if you will tell him what you do with your half hours he can tell you what your life is about. What are you doing with the half-hour drive to work and home each day? What do you do with the half hour you wait in the doctor's office? What about the half hour you wait for your meal to come in the restaurant? Do you have time in those half hours to show love to someone? Could you use those minutes to encourage someone by phone or letter? Could you pray for someone? Could you pray about what you can do for someone? Use the time to think creatively about what you have to give.

You could write a book in your half hours. You could win a soul. You could make a major decision in a half hour. A half hour could be the difference between a clean house and a dirty one. Your half hours are important, and you probably have a lot of them if you begin to look. Am I saying that you need to be doing something every second of the day? No, I am not saying that. In fact, you might decide you need to take a half hour and rest, and if you do that's okay, but at least you have used it on purpose rather than wasting it doing nothing.

Remember that every day that goes by is one you will never get back. Invest it; don't waste it.

Love with Your Thoughts, Words, and Possessions

The Power of Thoughts A woman shared this story to show the power of thoughts:

> During Christmas I moved a fig tree upstairs to the bedroom to make room for the Christmas tree. It had a small branch with about a dozen leaves on it down below the rest of the branches. It didn't look right, ruining the shape of the tree.
>
> When I would wake up in the morning I'd see that tree in the window and think, *I'm going to cut that branch off.* Every time I passed that tree I'd think, *That branch doesn't look right, I'm going to get rid of it.*
>
> Time went by. The tree was moved back to the living room. I continued to think a negative thought each time I noticed it. All total this lasted about a month and a half.
>
> One morning I walked by the tree and every leaf on that little branch was yellow. There was not one other yellow leaf on the whole tree. I got kind of goose bumpy and told my husband. He looked at me and said, "I'm sure glad you think *nice* things about me."
>
> I cut that branch off that day!
>
> I have always had a difficult relationship with my

mother-in-law. Of course I never thought I had any blame, being so sweet and all. I decided this was worth an experiment. Every time I thought about my mother-in-law I determined to bless her, to go out of my way to think about her and bless her!

She seldom calls me or has interest in chatting with me. But within five days she had called me three times—just for a moment, but they were friendly calls! She hadn't called me more than six times the whole last year.

This woman ordered my teaching series on the power of thoughts and said, "I watch what I think about other people now."

We think countless thoughts about other people, but we should do it more responsibly. I believe thoughts work in the spiritual realm, and although they cannot be seen with the naked eye, I do believe our thoughts are felt by other people. Just as the fig tree was negatively affected by the woman's negative thoughts, I believe people are affected by our thoughts.

What we think about people not only affects them, it also affects the way we treat them when we are around them. If I think secretly about how much I don't like someone and mentally go over all the faults I believe they have, when I see them I treat them according to the image I have formed in my mind.

One day I was shopping with my daughter, who was a teenager at the time. She had lots of pimples on her face that day and her hair was a mess. I remember thinking each time I looked at her, *You sure don't look very good today.* I noticed as the day wore on that she seemed to be depressed so I asked her what was wrong. She replied, "I just feel really ugly today." God taught me a lesson that day about the power of thoughts. We can help people with good, loving, and positive thoughts, but we can hurt them with evil, unloving, negative thoughts.

I encourage you to take a person a day as a prayer project and practice thinking good things about them on purpose. Throughout the day have some think sessions where you meditate on the strengths of the person, every good quality you can think of that they have, every favor they have ever done you, and any complimentary thing you can think of about their appearance. The next day, practice on another person, and keep rotating the important people in your life until you have formed a habit of thinking good things.

Love people with your thoughts, and as you do you will build them up and add strength to their life.

The Power of Words We have discussed how we can use words to build others up and to encourage and edify them, but I want to drive this point home as a way to love people. We all have the ability to use words to demonstrate love to others. Just yesterday I met a real estate agent who had beautiful blue eyes so I told her that her eyes were beautiful. I could tell it made her feel good about herself. And it cost only a moment of my time and a tiny bit of effort. I saw another agent who was unusually attractive so I told her she was very pretty, and she also responded in a very appreciative and pleased manner. I used my words to build two people up, and it all took place in the course of regular business activity. As Love Revolutionaries, we must use the power of words throughout each day to love and encourage those around us.

My husband came home from playing golf yesterday, and within five minutes he had told me that he loved me and that I looked nice and worked hard. I had been working on this book for about seven hours and was ready for a break, so his kind words made me feel loved and valuable. We went to dinner last night with our son and his wife and baby. I told Nicol that she is a good wife and mother. Right before that I saw my son whisper in her ear that he loved her. These are the kinds of things we should be saying to one another throughout the day as a way of loving and inspiring confidence.

The power of life and death is in the tongue. That is an amazing thought. We have authority to speak life or death to others and to ourselves. What we speak to others has an effect on our own lives. The Bible says, "The tongue has the power of life and death, and those who love it will eat its fruit" (Prov. 18:21 NIV).

Words are containers for power, and they can carry either creative or destructive power, as we choose. Choose your words carefully and speak them with caution. They convey messages that can be life altering. With our words we build or tear down a person's image of themselves. We can ruin someone's reputation with words, so be careful what you say about other people. Don't poison one person's attitude toward another.

Let's imagine your words are kept in a warehouse, and each morning you go there and peruse the shelves, selecting the words you will take with you that day as you go out into the world. You probably already know some of the people you will be with so you can select words in advance that will make them feel loved and give them confidence. Take words with you for everyone you run into throughout the day, and be prepared in your heart to be a blessing to every one of them by loving them with what you say.

Every day I want to see how many people I can lift up with my words. I've certainly wasted enough words in my life by speaking vain, useless things that either did nothing or made people feel badly. I am sorry for those wasted words, and I use my words now to undo the damage I have done in the past.

The tongue is a tiny muscle, but it can start destructive fires if we are not careful. King David prayed about the words of his tongue on a regularly basis. He said, "I will take heed and guard my ways, that I may sin not with my tongue" (Ps. 39:1). He prayed that the words of his mouth and the meditation of his heart would be acceptable and pleasing to God (see Ps. 19:14). He clearly knew the power of the tongue and realized he needed God's help to stay on the right path. We should follow David's example in that.

The Power of Possessions We all have possessions. Some have more than others, but all of us have something we can use as a tangible blessing to others. Thoughts and words are both wonderful and they help us show love, but possessions and material goods do the same thing, and for some people that is very important.

The Bible says if we have two coats we should share with him who has none and the same principle applies to our food (see Luke 3:11). The early Christian church that we see in the book of Acts was an amazingly powerful church that was growing daily. All kinds of supernatural signs and wonders and miracles were normal in their midst. The power of God was with them, and they showed love to one another with all their heart, mind, strength, and possessions.

> "Now the company of believers was of one heart and
> soul, and not one of them claimed that anything which

he possessed was [exclusively] his own, but everything
they had was in common and for the use of all."

Acts 4:32

Are we owners or stewards? Everything we have came from
God, and in reality it all belongs to Him. We are merely stewards of His property. Too often we grasp onto things too tightly.
We should hold them loosely so if God needs them they are
not difficult for us to let go of. Let's keep reminding ourselves
that possessions have no eternal value. What lasts is what we
do for others. Paul told the Corinthians that their gifts to the
poor would go on and endure forever throughout eternity (see
2 Cor. 9:9).

God wants us to enjoy our possessions, but He does not want
our possessions to possess us. Perhaps a good question to ask
ourselves regularly is: "Do I possess my possessions or do my
possessions possess me?" Are you able to use what you have to
bless people, or do you find it difficult to let go of things...even
things you are not using?

I receive perfume as a gift quite frequently, and since I
recently had a birthday the perfume bottles were abundant on
my shelf. One day I felt an urge to bless a friend who had done
me a favor and I remembered that she really liked one particular type of perfume that I wore. Of course I had a new bottle
with body lotion, and of course it was the most expensive one
on my shelf. I had to have a short talk with myself, but within a
few minutes I was able to get it off the shelf, into a gift bag, and
into her hands. It made her so happy and all it cost me was a
possession that could be replaced.

I implore you to start using your possessions to love people in tangible ways. Gifts are a wonderful way to show love. For example, once a friend told me my birthday gift would be late because it wasn't finished yet. When I finally received it I was surprised to find it was a hand painting of my dog, something I can look at and enjoy for many years. I am blessed by the painting, but even more blessed by the effort she made to finish it for me.

All giving is good, but as often as you can, make a special effort to get something into someone's hands that you know they really want. Just the fact that you listened enough to know that they liked and wanted that particular thing will bless them immensely. A friend of mine had a very special dog that died while still a puppy. She was heartbroken and could not afford to replace the dog, so I was able to get her one and surprise her. If we ask Him, God will enable us to provide for people as a means of showing love to them. He always provides plenty for us to keep and enjoy and plenty to give away, if we only hold things loosely and watch for opportunities to give.

Sometimes I go on what I call a giving rampage. I have a desire to be a blessing and want to use my possessions as a tangible way to show love so I go through my house, my drawers, my closet, and my jewelry chest to find things I can give away. I never fail to find things. It amazes me how I am tempted to hang onto them even though I may not have used an item for two or three years. We just like to own stuff! But how much better to use our possessions to be a blessing to someone else and make them feel loved and valuable.

If you are having difficulty seeing what you have to give, ask God to help you and you will quickly find that you have a wealth of things that can be used to show love to hurting people. As we use what we have for a good purpose love always increases, and other things are added to us as we show ourselves to be good stewards of God's possessions.

> [Remember] this: he who sows sparingly and
> grudgingly will also reap sparingly and grudgingly, and
> he who sows generously [that blessings may come to
> someone] will also reap generously and with blessings.
> Let each one [give] as he has made up his
> own mind and purposed in his heart, not
> reluctantly or sorrowfully or under compulsion,
> for God loves (He takes pleasure in, prizes
> above other things, and is unwilling to
> abandon or to do without) a cheerful
> (joyous, "prompt to do it") giver
> [whose heart is in his giving].
> *2 Corinthians 9:6–7*

When you are on your death bed, you will not ask for your bank account balance or an inventory of your possessions. You will want to be surrounded by family and friends who love you. Start building those relationships now by using all your resources to show love to people.

LOVE REVOLUTIONARY
Pastor Tommy Barnett

Revolution, *n* 1: the action by a celestial body of going around in an orbit 2: cycle 3: rotation 4: a sudden, radical, or complete change; esp, the overthrow of one government and the substitution of another by the governed.

Any and all of the dictionary definitions of revolution apply to your personal invitation to become part of the Love Revolution that God is expanding throughout the world.

In fact, the dictionary defines a revolutionary as one engaged in a revolution, or an adherent or advocate of revolutionary doctrines. The Love Revolution is truly a revolutionary doctrine, because the world views love as something that it must get and have, while Jesus is trying to revolutionize our thinking and our actions to define love as something that flows through us and that we must give away.

So, you are invited to participate in a unique circle of love! An ever-expanding circle with the center and circumference encompassing one goal: loving and encouraging people to follow Jesus Christ as we seek to welcome the world into God's family.

Our radical circle of love and encouragement includes the homeless, victims of natural and man-made disasters, victims of abuse and abusive relationships, women who are dealing with abortion issues and relational hurts, those who are economically disadvantaged or lack jobs, substance abusers and a multitude of those whose hurts are too vast to enumerate! So often in the past, churches have considered people such as these the dregs of humanity, but we are looking at them as the future treasures for God's kingdom.

The Love Revolution is simple: it begins with each one of us enlarging our circle of love to include those around us who are hurting. For many years, churches have emphasized programs to bring in new people. In alarming numbers, programs have come and gone, unsuccessful in creating enlargement. To the contrary, churches' spheres of influence have often become circles of diminishing size. Emphasizing programs over people has not accomplished the challenge of Jesus, who declared that we must love one another.

The Challenge of the Revolution

The cycle, the circle, or the Revolution of living like Jesus for other people is a challenge the apostle Paul set before us: "Therefore be imitators of God as dear children. And walk in love, as Christ also has loved us and given Himself for us, an offering and a sacrifice to God for a sweet-smelling aroma" (Eph. 5:1–2 NKJV).

This is the call of the Love Revolution: to walk in love, not just to decide to love. Many people know it's the right thing to love, but how do you enlarge your circle of love? It happens in a daily walk.

We all have a circle of influence, and we all belong in a circle. Most of us enjoy a circle of friends. What is the size of your circle? How inclusive or exclusive is it? I meet many well-meaning people who appear unaware of the minuscule size of their circle. If we are living out "the Christ mentality," and the mind of Christ is within us, each circle must exclude no one and include everyone.

Important to me, and defining my personal circle, is the issue of sinners I'm challenged to bring into my circle. I find it easy to get my hatred of sin mixed up with the sinner, causing me to hate the sinner because I abhor the sin. I have learned that God intends me to hate the sin, but love the sinner. Sometimes, our attitude toward sin can be like an encounter with a dangerous rattlesnake confronting a child. The snake is coiled and ready to strike. We hate the snake, but love the child and want to rescue the child from the fangs of potential death.

We are compelled to warn people of the consequences of sin, but we also must move in the compassion of the Lord to include sinners in my circle of love. Besides, most sinners are aware of the negative effects of wrongful choices in their life. And they don't need someone else to come along and condemn them. Many are already tormented by the belief that the church, let alone God, will not welcome them because of their lifestyle, addictions, unfaithfulness, or gross mistakes.

People in leadership often ask us why our church in Phoenix and the Dream Center in Los Angeles purposely work with the disenfranchised, the unlovely, and the unwanted. They have made poor choices. I have never doubted God intended everyone to be in His circle of love.

If we are what we profess to be, true expressions of Jesus Christ, no one can be excluded. That includes people of different doctrines, denominations, and experiences. We must be encouragers, heralds of hope, that point people toward the unconditional love of God, and then become an evidence of it ourselves toward them.

I am not responsible for those who exclude me or include

me. I'm responsible for myself, and whom I exclude. Jesus, in that universal statement when He hung on the cross said basically, "Father, forgive them because they don't know what they are doing" (see Luke 23:34). His circle included those who crucified Him. Even His critics who mocked Him and spit on Him and cruelly offered vinegar when He asked for water are included in His circle of love.

Our circle exists to include even those who wronged us. I have learned to never fight with people in my circle. There is no battle. I am safe as long as I include all in my circle of love. Then I will not be hurt.

You cannot make too many friends, but if you have an enemy, you'll encounter that enemy wherever you go. What you hate, you're tied to. By accepting everyone, you begin mastering what the love of God is about. Whoever is outside your circle of love can hurt you, but whoever is inside of your circle of love will not hurt you.

The legalistic standard of religion that some often hold high is narrow and exclusive. The standard of the Love Revolution is universal. Love heals! Love restores! Love illuminates! Love lifts! The larger my circle of love gets, the happier I am and the more I can exhibit the love of God to others.

A Love Revolution in Action

When we first started the Los Angeles Dream Center, we purposefully went into an unloved area that government, churches, and even the police had abandoned as hopeless. Because we enlarged our circle of love to include gang members, runaways, the homeless, prostitutes, hardened criminals, and rejected young people, our circle of love has been enlarged to the point that Dream Centers around the world reach out to the unwanted and the unloved, displaying the love of Christ through acts of service.

Every week, hundreds of volunteers from the Los Angeles Dream Center's Adopt-a-Block outreach (one of hundreds of aspects of the Love Revolution going out from the Dream Center) go out into the neighborhoods and simply serve their neighbors by cleaning up their yards, painting over graffiti, and serving them in a variety of ways. It's just serving people they don't even know to show the love of Christ.

And at a time when crime and social degradation has increased throughout the city of Los Angeles, the neighborhood near the Dream Center has seen a drop of over 70 percent in the crime rate, while multitudes have come to faith in Christ. The Rampart division, a neighborhood notorious for its corruption, crime, and sin is now a shining example of people walking out the love of Christ. That's a Love Revolution!

Forgiving and For Giving

Have you been forgiven? Then forgive others. Love is forgiving, and love is for giving.

Giving love is one of the most difficult things to do. In many ways it's more difficult than giving money, because love has to come from an open heart. There is no way to just make it a cold business transaction.

But many of us misunderstand what love is. We think it's something we can receive and possess like a gift or something owed. But that's not what love really is.

Love is something you can only give, not something you possess. None of us own love—we use love. The biblical word for love is in the active voice, meaning that love not given is not love at all.

Have you ever met someone who is always needing love, but never getting enough? The more they focus on the love they feel they deserve, the less love they seem to have. They are so focused on their lack that their supply is never enough.

When helping hurting people, we meet people all the time who tell us they just want to be loved by someone. I have discovered the opposite is true: we don't need to be loved as much as we need to love someone.

When we love unconditionally, we can never become imprisoned to a man or woman. But when we demand that somebody love us, we become their slave and are easily imprisoned by their lack of love toward us.

More Important to Give Than to Receive

I believe it's more important for people to show love than to receive it. When you show love, it turns on the heavenly faucet from which God pours love continually on us; the more love you show, the more you have and the easier it is to leave the tap on and let it flow to others.

The amount of love you have is directly influenced by how much love you give. It's a paradox, but it's true: the only way to hold on to love is to give it away.

> The only way to hold on to love is to give it away.

If you constantly give love away, you're always focused on what you have to give, and that supply will grow. Even if no one loves you back, you'll have an endless supply of love through Jesus, and your life will be full of love.

When I was young, I loved people less than I do now. But I tried giving love away and found that my own supply expanded. As long as I keep using the love I have, God continues giving me deeper love.

As a young man, I didn't truly love the little children—I only appreciated them. But one day I made a choice to love them. Today my heart overflows with love for little children. I can say now that I genuinely love and enjoy children, and I love to bless them.

I enjoy life tremendously now, but when I was a young preacher I wasn't nearly as joyful. I have twenty times the joy now that I did twenty years ago. I made up my mind that I could choose to be dreary or joyful, and I may as well choose joy. I have found more joy coming to me since I decided to give it away.

Part of the Love Revolution coming to the body of Christ is to help people see that pursuing love is the wrong way to go about it. We must help people, through our example, to realize that to have love, you don't seek it, you give it.

True love doesn't come from any person; it comes from God. Even my love for my wife, Marja, is pure because I found the source. We learned it is more blessed to give love than to receive it, and when a husband and wife actively give love to each other, they'll have a great marriage.

When the body of Christ learns to actively give love to a lost and dying world, we will enlarge our circle of love and influence our society for the better, and we'll improve our society.

Are you ready for the Revolution? Here are a few suggestions to walk out the love of Christ in your personal version of the Love Revolution:

1. Speak love. Come right out and say it.
Become a "love waterfall," always pouring it on other people. Some people say, "I'm not wired that way." If every believer said, "I love you" more, it would redefine the world's relationships. Try it. If you tell people you love them, you'll hear it back. When you say, in a heartfelt manner, the words "I love you" it empowers you in the love of Christ.

2. Put your love in writing.
I keep an "I love you" file for the nice letters I get. They mean a lot to me. A simple note of encouragement from you can mean a great deal to someone else. Writing down your love makes it permanent and lasting. It could even be a life preserver to someone if they are ever drowning in despair. Writing someone a message of the love of God encourages them, inspires you, and increases an awareness of God's love.

3. Risk doing outrageously loving things.
When we go above and beyond what others may expect of us to express the love of Christ, the results of those loving actions are multiplied in the lives of others. Sometimes, it takes a little risk to do a little more—that's part of the Love Revolution. Ask yourself, "Can I do a little more than I presently am in loving others?" Make your life memorable; revolutionaries always do outrageous things. Make an otherwise ordinary day extraordinary by letting your love be outrageous in its expression of the love of God.

4. Love takes a willingness to rejoice and weep.

Frequently showing love is about helping someone who's in no mood to celebrate. Sharing grief with someone, or walking through the valley with them, lays deep foundations of love and trust. Jesus went to weddings and funerals. He knew what people needed in both circumstances. We must share the love of God in all circumstances so that we are comfortable showing love to the joyful and to the mourning.

5. Learn to love different people in different ways.

People receive and give love differently, so we must learn to love people in different ways. It is vital for each one of us to learn how to give and receive love with those close to us, and it is imperative that we learn how to give love to those in the world around us, especially those who may not receive love from anyone else. Study people and the Word of God, see how Jesus loved people and you will learn to show love to different people in different ways that makes everyone feel great and brings glory to God.

Want to Be a Revolutionary?

So, will you act like a revolutionary today? Will each and every day of your life from now on have evidence that you are part of the Love Revolution? What is it that you will be remembered for? Your wit? Your intelligence? In the end, it's only love that matters. Love is what gives us eternal value. Everyone wants to be recognized as spiritual creatures made in the image of God, and love is the only way to do that.

Love as if your love is unlimited, and you'll find that it is. You may not love someone when you first meet that person, but if you give the love you have, it will grow.

I challenge you to be the "lovingest" person you know, and I can tell you in advance that if you love at all times, your supply will never run dry.

So what do you say? Re-enlist in the army of God that He is raising up today and I'll see you in the Love Revolution!

CHAPTER
15

Do We Need Revival or a Revolution?

Everyone thinks of changing the world, but no
one thinks of changing himself.
Leo Tolstoy

When something is revived, the old is brought to life again,
renewed attention is brought to something. When society experiences renewed religious interest, it is called revival. Merriam-
Webster's Collegiate Dictionary defines *revival* as "an often highly
emotional evangelistic meeting or series of meetings." All of my
adult life as a Christian, I have heard people talk about and pray
for revival. But I am no longer sure that revival is what we need.
I think we need something far more radical. I think we need a
Revolution. Webster's dictionary defines the word *revolution* as
"a sudden, radical, or complete change."

Somehow we are more comfortable with redressing the old
than we are with radical change. But have past revivals transformed the church and the world? They have certainly been

beneficial in their time, but what do we need right now in the church so we can be effective in the world? What is it going to take for us to be the light Christ has called us to be?

In his book *The Barbarian Way*, Erwin McManus writes, "Let go of sanitized Christianity and get back to the powerful, raw and ancient faith that chooses revolution over compromise, peril over safety, and passion over lukewarm and watered-down religions." Christ's passion drove Him to the cross. Will ours at least drive us to sacrifice some of our old ways so the next generation might experience the transforming power of Revolutionary Love?

Jesus was a revolutionary, and He certainly was not an advocate of tradition. He came to bring change, and it upset the religious people of His day. God never changes, but He does change others. I have found that He loves creativity and new things and He keeps things fresh and on fire.

Some churches will not even consider changing something as simple as the style of their music. They will sing hymns and play only the organ as long as they exist. They ignore the fact that their congregations keep shrinking in size and are not affecting their community at all. They need to look around on Sunday morning and ask why everyone in the building is middle aged or older. Where are the young people? Where is the enthusiasm? Where is the life?

Several years ago, we began to experience a slight decline in the conferences we do around the nation and noticed that most everyone attending was middle aged or older. Our son, who was twenty-four years old at the time, started encouraging us to make some radical changes in music styles, lighting, decor, and our manner of dress. He said that his generation desperately needed to be reached with the gospel of Jesus Christ, but it was turned off by old-style religion that had a reputation for being legalistic and boring. For about a year, Dave and I were both very resistant. We said what most people say when they don't want to change: "God doesn't change." We also felt that what we had done so far had worked well. Why change it? A lot of pride was involved, and it was difficult to let a twenty-four-year-old who had just come to work with us tell us what we should do. But as the year went by we began to listen to other younger people, and we realized we did not need to worship methods. Our message would not change, but the package it came in needed to change.

The world changes, people change, new generations think differently than previous ones, and we need to be concerned about how to reach them. I wanted to see young people at my conferences, but I was not willing to provide anything that would interest them. I wasn't willing to meet them where they were. But little by little our hearts were opened to try new things, and we saw great results. Not only did we not lose the people we had, but new ones came, and many of them were young and enthusiastic. If we have the wisdom of the older generation and the enthusiastic creativity of the younger one, then we have the best of both worlds.

One day we held a business meeting with our leadership team at the office. Our son, who had been pressing for change, had an idea about something and I disagreed with him. He kept pressing his point so I asked everyone else what they thought and they all agreed with me. When I made the point that everyone in the room agreed with me, our son Dan said, "Of course they all agree with you, Mom—they are all your age." At that point I began to realize that I had surrounded myself with people like me and by doing so I was blocking variety. We needed to have leaders of all ages, not just people who were all from the same generation.

On another occasion Dan wanted to use some colors in our monthly magazine that we had never used before. I did not like them so I said no. He was aggressive about using new colors, and I emphatically said, "I don't like them, and we are not going to use them!" He said, "I did not realize you were called to minister to *yourself*. What if other people do like those colors?" At that point I had an eye-opening experience. I realized that I had dress codes at the office that were what *I* liked and we used colors in the magazine, on advertisements, and in the building that *I* liked. We had the music that *I* liked. I was ashamed when I realized how many of my decisions were all about what I liked and was comfortable with, not about what people needed.

Dave and I both began to realize that we were worshipping methods and that those methods meant absolutely nothing to God. It was His message He wanted to get out, and the package it came in could certainly be changed. So we started to change and have continued to be open to change ever since. We have changed our dress styles to a more contemporary style. We changed our worship bands to those that would draw in more young people. I decided to love the current generation enough to sing songs they could enjoy. We shortened the length of our services because our whole society today wants to do things quicker. I was accustomed to three-hour church services, but not everyone is, so we decided to meet people in the middle. We changed our lighting to be more aggressive. We even got a fog machine that they tell me creates atmosphere. I still think it only hinders people from being able to see clearly, but I can handle fog if it gets people to relate to me enough to listen to the gospel message. Remember that Paul said he became whatever he needed to be in order to win people to the gospel of Jesus Christ (see 1 Cor. 9:20–22). He did not worship methods and neither should we.

The Bible says that in the last days we will experience a church that is selfish and self-centered. People will be loose in morals and they will hold a form of religion but deny the power of the gospel (see 2 Tim. 3:1–5). We need to see God's power in our churches. We need to see changed lives, healing, restoration, and redemption. We need to see the love of God flowing freely. We need to see a Revolution, and I am determined to be part of it!

I can honestly say that a lot of the changes we have made to our conferences are not ones that I particularly like. But I am learning more every day that love requires us to let go of our ways and find out what God's ways are for the current season. A lot of our changes have definitely been a sacrifice for me personally, but I know in my heart they have all been the right thing to do. As foolish as it sounds, there was a time when I actually thought God would not bless someone if they were on the platform trying to lead the people while wearing denim. Then I seriously thought about what Moses was probably wearing when he went to the mountain to receive the Ten Commandments and I finally realized how foolish I was being. John the Baptist was a strange dresser, he had weird eating habits, and his address was the wilderness, but he led a revolution. He prepared the way for the Messiah. He was not a fan of organized religion and he called the most religious leaders of his day a brood of vipers. He was sickened by the self-righteous religious people of his day who went to the temple to pray but would not lift a finger to help anyone in need.

God looks on the heart, and we need to learn to do the same thing. He was not concerned about the way Moses or John looked. He was thrilled to find someone who was not afraid to lead a revolt against dead religion and lead people into intimacy with Him.

Love Sacrifices

The word *sacrifice* is not one that usually excites us because it means to give up something we might prefer to keep. In the original language of the New Testament (Greek) the word means "an act of offering, or that which is offered." Love does not insist on its own way (see 1 Cor. 13:5). Love often requires us to sacrifice our way of doing something.

In the Old Testament "sacrifice" referred to animals sacrificed for sin, but in the New Testament it refers to Christ's sacrifice of Himself on the cross. The New Testament also urges believers to "offer your bodies as living sacrifices, holy and pleasing to God—this is your spiritual act of worship" (Rom. 12:1).

The main reason we don't see as much real love in the world as we should is because people don't like to sacrifice. Our natural tendency is to keep, not to give sacrificially. We protect our comfort zone. We might give if it is easy or convenient, but when sacrifice is required, we draw back. How many of your ways are you desperately hanging onto without ever asking, "Does God have a different way for me to do this?" After all, the Bible says that His ways are higher than our ways (see Isa. 55:8).

Thankfully we can form new habits and actually live a sacrificial life and enjoy it. When we remember to do kindness to others and refuse to neglect being generous, the Bible says that God is pleased with such sacrifices (see Heb. 13:16). "God so loved the world that he gave his one and only Son" (John 3:16). Love must give, and giving requires sacrifice!

We all have a way that we like to do things, and we usually think that our way is the right way. One of the huge problems with religion in general is that it often gets stuck in "old ways" that are no longer truly ministering to people, but it refuses to change. It refuses to sacrifice its ways.

A friend recently told me that she makes her teenage daughters go to church every Sunday but that they are always bored and cannot wait for the service to be over. She admitted that they get absolutely nothing out of being there. These girls probably love God but don't relate to the methods being used by the church. They are from a new generation that does things a new way. Sadly, many children raised in Christian homes turn from any kind of religion when they become adults. They may have been discouraged by hypocrisy, turned off by legalistic rules, or been bored to tears. Church did not work for them. They wanted something genuine and powerful, something fun and adventurous, but they ended up with a long list of things they could not do.

Tommy Barnett, who co-founded the Los Angeles Dream Center, discovered that a lot of the young people in that area skateboard. When he heard that a famous skater was coming into the area to film a movie and that a $50,000 half-pipe had been erected for the movie, he asked boldly if the church could have it when the movie was finished. They gave it to him, it was moved to the Dream Center, and now on Saturdays anyone who has attended a service that week gets a ticket to skateboard if they want one. Pastor Barnett's willingness to do something radical and new has brought thousands of teenagers to the Dream Center to skate. And many of those teenagers end up accepting Christ. He sacrificed old traditions that might not have allowed such a thing in order to reach skaters with love. He understood their desire and helped them fulfill it. We cannot expect young people—or any people, for that matter—to only want to read the Bible and pray. People need to laugh and have fun and adventure, and they should not have to go to the world to do it.

Pastor Barnett said when his two hundred voice white-robed choir sang "How Great Thou Art," the teenagers went to sleep, so when the teens asked if they could sing some of their music the next week, he gave them permission. As he listened the following week, he realized they had converted a rock 'n' roll song into a spiritual song. At first he thought, *Oh no. What have I done?* But then as he listened he realized that God's blessing was on the song. It is amazing what God will use that we would reject. God sees the heart behind it.

I believe we must learn that only the message of the gospel is sacred, not the methods we use to present it. If we don't learn that, we are in danger of being irrelevant to the current generation and losing them. They desperately need to know the love of God, and we may have to sacrifice our ways to help make it happen.

When we made changes in our conferences, did we sacrifice what the present congregation wanted for the sake of those we wanted to see come? Were we being unfair to those who had been with us a long time? I don't think we were because those who are more mature spiritually should be ready and willing to sacrifice to see others know the truth. When I explained to people why I was making changes, they all cheered. People want to do what is right; they just need understanding. Of course, there will always be people who resist change, and those people get left behind. They stay where they are, but God continues to move forward with or without them.

When we speak of the need for a Love Revolution, we are speaking of radical change in the way we do life. We should be asking God daily what we can do for Him, not just what He can do for us. Anyone participating in a Love Revolution will be required to make sacrifices for the sake of others, but those sacrifices will also bring a new joy. Our focus must change from ourselves to others. We need to think about what we can give, not what we can get. When Jesus traveled with His disciples, He taught them about life. I believe we need to hear messages from our pulpits about how to live daily life in a way that is pleasing to God, not just messages on doctrinal issues. We need to make sure the messages are relevant to all generations.

Have you known Christ for a long time and yet His love is still imprisoned in you? If so, it is time to boldly let it out. We are to be channels for God's love to flow through, not reservoirs. Make yourself available daily for God's use. I dare you to pray this prayer daily, "God, show me what I can do for You today."

God wants us to present ourselves daily as a living sacrifice (see Rom. 12:1). He wants us to offer all of our faculties and resources to Him. A Love Revolution will require sacrifices of time, energy, finances, our ways, and many other things, but to live without love is to sacrifice the life that Jesus died to give us.

Get Out of That Religious Rut

Are you ready to get out of your religious rut and get involved with real people who have real problems? The key to happiness is not in being loved; it is in having someone to love. If you really want to be happy, find somebody to love. If you want to put a smile on God's face, then find a hurting person and help them.

I went to church for thirty years without ever hearing one sermon on my biblical responsibility to care for orphans, widows, the poor, and the oppressed. I was shocked when I finally realized how much of the Bible is about helping other people. I spent most of my Christian life thinking the Bible was about how God could help me. It's no wonder I was unhappy.

I am currently preparing for a trip to Africa to visit Ethiopia, Rwanda, and Uganda. I know I will see need there that is greater than anything I have seen anywhere, and I am ready and eager to give. The trip will be a sacrifice of time, energy, comfort, and finances, but I need to go. I need to touch hurting people. I need to get close to poverty and starvation, so close that I will never forget it after I return home.

I will hold babies that are malnourished from starvation, and I will see the pain in their mothers' eyes that is there from watching their children die and not being able to do anything about it. But I will also help some of them. Perhaps I can't help all of them, but I will do what I can because I refuse to do nothing! I will be able to come back and share firsthand with the friends and partners of our ministry how they can get involved and help people.

People want to help, but many just don't know what to do. They need someone to organize it for them. Do you have leadership skills? If you do, why not organize an outreach to the poor in your city or initiate a way for you and your friends to get involved in missions to the poor and lost around the world? One group of women who were determined to do something collected "stuff" from their neighbors and had a huge garage sale and gave all the money to help the poor. They were so successful that they kept doing it, and now they have an actual store that is run by volunteers. All the merchandise for sale is donated and all the money is given to missions. They were able to give sixty-five thousand dollars in one year alone. (By the way, most of the women are over sixty years old, and I am so proud of them for doing something so creative and valuable. They have decided to let their latter years be among their most fruitful.)

Be determined to help someone. Be creative! Lead a revolt against living in a religious rut where you go to church and go home and go back to church but you're not really helping anybody. Don't just sit in church pews and sing hymns. Get involved in helping hurting people. Remember the words of Jesus:

> "I was hungry and you gave Me no food; I was thirsty and you gave Me no drink; I was a stranger and you did not take Me in, naked and you did not clothe Me, sick and in prison and you did not visit Me."
>
> Then they also will answer Him, saying, "Lord, when did we see You hungry or thirsty or a stranger or naked or sick or in prison, and did not minister to You?"
>
> Then He will answer them, saying, "Assuredly, I say to you, inasmuch as you did not do *it* to one of the least of these, you did not do *it* to Me."
>
> *Matthew 25:42–45* NKJV

I take up compassion and **surrender** my excuses.
I stand against injustice
and **commit** to live out simple acts of God's love.
I refuse to do nothing. This is my resolve.
I AM THE LOVE REVOLUTION.

NOTES

1. **What in the World Is Wrong?**

   1. "Help End Sex Trafficking!" http://www.crisisaid.org/traf
   fickstats.html
   2. "Hunger Facts: International," http://www.bread.org/
   learn/hunger-basics/hunger-facts-international.html

3. **Nothing Good Happens Accidentally**

   1. "Forced to Flee: Uganda's Young 'Night Commuters',"
   http://www.theirc.org/where/page-28828228.html
   2. "Simple Statistics"

6. **Overcome Evil with Good**

   1. "Widows in Third World Nations," http://www.deathref
   erence.com
   2. "Uganda, Ghana and Cote d'Ivoire—The situation of
   widows," http://www.ifad.org/gender/learning/challenges/
   widows/55.htm

7. **Justice for the Oppressed**

   1. "Prostitution is not a choice, it is a lack of choices," http://
   www.spokesmanreview.com/blogs/vox/media/Feb07vox
   page2.pdf

9. Make People Feel Valuable

1. George W. Crane, *Dr. Crane's Radio Talks*, vol. 1 (Mellot, IN: Hopkins Syndicate, Inc., 1948), 7.
2. Ibid., 8–9.
3. Ibid., 16.
4. Original source unknown.
5. Attributed to William Penn and Stephen Grellet.

12. Unconditional Love

1. http://preventdisease.com/home/weeklywellness203.shtml

ABOUT THE AUTHOR

JOYCE MEYER is one of the world's leading practical Bible teachers. A #1 *New York Times* bestselling author, she has written more than eighty inspirational books, including *100 Ways to Simplify Your Life, Never Give Up!*, the entire Battlefield of the Mind family of books, and two novels. *The Penny and Any Minute*, as well as many others. She has also released thousands of audio teachings, as well as a complete video library. Joyce's *Enjoying Everyday Life*® radio and television programs are broadcast around the world, and she travels extensively conducting conferences. Joyce and her husband, Dave, are the parents of four grown children and make their home in St. Louis, Missouri.

JOYCE MEYER MINISTRIES
U.S. & FOREIGN OFFICE ADDRESSES

Joyce Meyer Ministries
P.O. Box 655
Fenton, MO 63026
USA
(636) 349-0303
www.joycemeyer.org

Joyce Meyer Ministries—Canada
P.O. Box 7700
Vancouver, BC V6B 4E2
CANADA
(800) 868-1002

Joyce Meyer Ministries—Australia
Locked Bag 77
Mansfield Delivery Centre
Queensland 4122
AUSTRALIA
(07) 3349 1200

Joyce Meyer Ministries—England
P.O. Box 1549
Windsor SL4 1GT
UNITED KINGDOM
01753 831102

Joyce Meyer Ministries—South Africa
P.O. Box 5
Cape Town 8000
SOUTH AFRICA
(27) 21-701-1056

OTHER BOOKS BY JOYCE MEYER

Any Minute

Never Give Up

The Secret to True Happiness

New Day, New You Devotional

I Dare You

The Penny

The Power of Simple Prayer

The Everyday Life Bible

The Confident Woman

Look Great, Feel Great

Battlefield of the Mind*

Battlefield of the Mind Devotional

Battlefield of the Mind for Teens

Battlefield of the Mind for Kids

Approval Addiction

Ending Your Day Right

21 Ways to Finding Peace and Happiness

The Secret Power of Speaking God's Word

Seven Things That Steal Your Joy

Starting Your Day Right

Beauty for Ashes (revised edition)

How to Hear from God*

Managing Your Emotions

Healing the Brokenhearted

*Me and My Big Mouth!**

Prepare to Prosper

Do It Afraid!

Expect a Move of God in Your Life . . . Suddenly!

*Enjoying Where You Are on the
Way to Where You Are Going*

A New Way of Living

When, God, When?

Why, God, Why?

The Word, the Name, the Blood

Tell Them I Love Them

Peace

*If Not for the Grace of God**

Joyce Meyer Spanish Titles

*Las Siete Cosas Que Te Roban el Gozo
(Seven Things That Steal Your Joy)*

Empezando Tu Día Bien (Starting Your Day Right)

* Study Guide available for this title.

Books by Dave Meyer

Life Lines